HOME PICKLING

T0352742

Cooks eager to rediscover the lost culinary art of pickling will be well served by this fascinating and informative text, written by the founder of the best-known vinegar and pickling company in the United Kingdom. Beginning with an explanation of the history of pickling, principles and advantages, the book goes on to give detailed instructions on the preservation of artichokes, beans, beetroot, cabbage, shallots, tomatoes, peaches, cherries, a wide variety of chutneys and ketchups, meats and many other foods. Instructions are also given for mixing spices and determining correct levels of acidity and brine.

THE KEGAN PAUL LIBRARY OF CULINARY ARTS

Editorial Advisor
Peter Hopkins

All About Ices, Jellies and Creams • Henry G. Harris and S. P. Borella

Alexander Dumas' Dictionary of Cuisine • Alexander Dumas

Dictionary of Cooking

Something New in Sandwiches • *M. Redington White*

Three Hundred and Sixty-Six Menus and Twelve Hundred Recipes • *Baron Brisse*

A Guide to the Greedy by A Greedy Woman • Elizabeth Robins Pennell

Book of the Table • *M. Auguste Kettner*

Chinese Cookery Secrets • *Esther Chan*

Food for the Greedy • *Nancy Shaw*

French Household Cooking • *Frances Keyzer*

Good Living • Saravan Buren

Home Pickling • *Henry Sarson*

Moorish Recipes • John Fourth Marquis of Bute

Mrs. A. B. Marshall\s Cookery Book • *B. Marshall*

Paris Bistro Cookery • *Alexander Watt*

The Country Housewife's Book • *Lucy H. Yates*

The Finer Cooking • *X. M. Boulestin*

The Jam Book • *May Byron*

The Modern Cook • Charles Elme Francatelli

The South American Gentleman's Companion • *Charles H. Baker*

What Shall We Have To-Day? • *X. Marcel Boulestin*

A King's Confectioner in the Orient • *Friedrich Unger*

Skuse's Complete Confectioner • *E. Skuse*

The Gentle Art of Cookery • Hilda Leyel and Olga Hartley

All About Genoese, Petits Fours, Glaces and Bon Bons • *H. G. Harris and S. P. Borella*

HOME PICKLING

Henry Sarson

Routledge
Taylor & Francis Group

LONDON AND NEW YORK

DEDICATION

To all those housewives who have forgotten or never knew how to make pickles like mother used to make ; to the enthusiastic diggers of allotments whose surplus onions lie rotting in a corner of the toolshed ; to affluent owners of greenhouses whose final crop of tomatoes the fickle English sun failed to ripen, or to anyone else interested in preserving food from waste and in varying its monotony, this book is dedicated.

H. S.

FOREWORD

I AM happy to contribute a foreword to this timely little book, which shows how the fruits of the earth can be preserved by pickling for the winter days ahead.

Who does not remember our mother's store-cupboard and her pride in it? In days gone by, many of the good things in the cupboard of farm and cottage were pickled. But lately the art of pickling—for it is an art—has fallen into neglect. We shall do well to revive it now. We need to turn to vegetables as a mainstay of our diet in war-time. We shall benefit in health and ease the task of our shipping. Pickling is one method of putting by the surplus of the season for use when supplies are scarce.

Every housewife can help the country by saving food. This little book will prove a useful guide.

Woolton.

15th April 1940.

CONTENTS

HOME PICKLING

CHAPTER I

WHAT IS PICKLING?

" How I luxuriously thirst for noble pickle."
Martial. Book XIII.

BEFORE express trains and turbine steamers brought the Mediterranean to our back doors or turned the Antipodes into one huge larder, pickling was of supreme importance to every household. Winters were long and grim, fresh vegetables practically unprocurable, whilst for months on end fruit was unknown to masses of the people.

Winter diet largely consisted of pickled food in various forms : salted and smoked meats such as beef, pork, bacon and hams; pickled and salted fish, especially herrings and a wide range of what we understand to-day by pickles ; vegetables and fruits preserved in vinegar and spices.

The stillroom one constantly finds reference to in old cookery books was the household factory and stores. Here the industrious housewife made her preserves, brewed the beer, cider, perry or mead, and put down her pickles. It was her ability and pride to guard against the possibility of future want, if not actual famine, by having always on hand ample supplies of preserved and pickled foods, and very well she seems to have done it judging by the recipes and menus handed down to us.

As the population of the country increased and the towns grew into cities and the villages into towns, providing food for the people became an industry and the household ceased to be a self-contained unit. The butcher, baker and candlestick-maker became people of local and finally national importance, with a corresponding decrease in strictly household-produced foods. This tendency was very marked with what is roughly called the industrial revolution. Cheap and efficient transport as developed by the railways made fresh fish available everywhere, and fish pickling was the first to die a natural death. Yet pickled fish were eaten in every household barely a hundred years ago, every little sea-coast village possessed some sort of fish-pickler, and even such remote districts as the Cotswolds pickled and cured salmon and trout. To-day the only relic we have in our diet is a Bismarck herring used as an hors d'œuvres and an occasional soused herring or mackerel. Except for epicures the others are unobtainable !

The next great blow at home pickling was the discovery and development of canning, and this was quickly followed by its ally in mass food production, refrigeration. Both of these have been of immense value to the diet of the people, but like all good things they can be overdone. Mass production means monotony, and it is so simple when the unexpected guest arrives to pop round the corner and buy something tasty in a tin. Yet your great-grandmother would not have had to pop, she would have had that something tasty in her stillroom or larder and would have been saved at least the agony of a gashed thumb from a tin-opener that won't work.

To-day there are definite signs of revolt against this state of affairs, noticeably so in the greatly increased jam-making at home (for jams are only fresh fruit pickled in sugar), whilst a glance at the women's magazines and women's pages in the newspapers show that a new interest is being taken in food and its variation.

Yet the very blessings that science has brought us through transport, canning and refrigeration have made variation more difficult for the average housewife. Our chief meats are still beef, mutton, pork and bacon, and indeed in flesh foods there has been a decrease in variety. Venison is practically unheard of to-day, whilst game and wild-fowl are strictly preserved and available in limited quantities only.

Luckily this does not apply to vegetables and fruits. Our ancestors had nothing approaching the supply or variety we enjoy, but what they had they used to good purposes.

In 1747, Mrs. Hannah Glasse published her celebrated *Domestic Cookery Made Easy*. It quickly ran through a number of editions, and contains a vast amount of instruction and detail on all branches of domestic science, including the first real attempt to describe the art of pickling.

There are, of course, many earlier references to pickling, but they are usually isolated recipes lacking in detail and with little application to-day.

Hannah, however, knew her job, and many of her recipes have been copied with but slight alteration in the legion of cookery books that has appeared since.

She seems to have had a free run for some years, but about 1820 a rival appeared in *Domestic Cookery*, by A Lady. This was published anonymously and must have been popular, for copies may still be picked up for a few pence on second-hand bookstalls.

These good ladies, though they dealt with pickling at some length, had no real knowledge of what it was scientifically. Their recipes were based on experience, the test of trial and error. They knew that certain processes produced certain results and never troubled to ask " why." If something went wrong and the pickles turned mouldy, it was just too bad. You must try again next year and boil them a little longer or use stronger vinegar.

Unfortunately we cannot follow that system to-day. A hundred and fifty years ago the housewife had ample time, ample space and ample domestic help; but the modern, rather harassed wife who tries to make pickles in a small suburban kitchen, only to have them go wrong, is not likely to waste time and money on a second attempt.

Let us hope that after reading these pages her first attempt will fully repay her for her trouble.

Wasted foods cry out to be pickled.

These organisms are divided into three groups.

CHAPTER II

OF WAYS AND MEANS

" Vinegar, spice and all things nice."
Old Nursery Rhyme.

SUCCESS in anything means understanding what you are trying to do and how to do it. At the risk, therefore, of boredom we must look at the scientific side of pickling; but as the average housewife is not a doctor of science, as simple language as possible will be used.

Food goes bad chiefly for one reason. It is attacked by minute organisms which, under suitable conditions, grow at a rapid rate and break down the composition of that particular food. These organisms are divided into three groups—bacteria (which are the smallest), yeasts and moulds, and they usually work in that order. The vast majority are quite harmless in themselves and many are beneficial and are used industrially. It is only when the wrong one gets into the wrong food that trouble arises.

For instance, the blue mould that makes Stilton Cheese so delicious becomes a very unwelcome visitor on a bunch of hot-house grapes, and the lactic bacteria that turn your milk sour would also turn it into cream cheese if you'd let them.

Home Pickling is so treating the food that these organisms cannot grow and it becomes pickled or preserved.

There are three natural preservatives: sugar, salt and vinegar. Sugar is chiefly used to preserve fruits as jams, marmalades and jellies; salt is the main agent in preserving meats and fish; whilst vinegar plays the principal part in turning vegetables and fruits into pickles—though salt is an important partner in first brining the vegetables, and sugar is also used when sweet pickles or chutneys are made.

All three work in the same way. They are used in such a concentration that the organisms which would start up putrefaction are either killed or weakened so that the food is preserved.

But success or failure depends entirely on getting this right concentration. Everyone is familiar with the simple test in jam-making of pouring a spoonful on to a cold plate to see if it sets, whilst all know that " runny " jam is liable to ferment.

Unfortunately in pickles there is no such simple test, yet the acidity of the finished pickle must be in the region of 3 per cent. if the pickles are to keep, and it is due to it falling below this (often very much below) that practically all the failures in home-made pickles can be traced.

There is a simple explanation of this fact, but one which is rarely understood. All fruits and vegetables are mainly composed of water. A glance down the following table will show how high their water content is:

PERCENTAGES OF WATER IN FRUITS AND VEGETABLES

Subject	Average percentage of water	Subject	Average percentage of water
Apples	. 84	Lettuce	. 95
Asparagus	. 95	Marrow	. 93–95
Beans	. 68–70	Mushrooms	. 88
Beetroot	. 88	Onions	. 87–89
Brussels Sprouts	. 83	Pears	. 83
Cabbage (Red)	. 93	Peas	. 74–77
Cabbage (White)	. 94	Plums	. 81
Carrots	. 88	Potatoes	. 78
Cauliflower	. 90–92	Radish	. 76–91
Celery	. 94	Raspberries	. 84
Cherries	. 79	Runner Beans	. 89
Cucumber	. 95–97	Strawberries	. 87
Gooseberries	. 85	Tomato	. 94

The usual strength of draught vinegar is 4 per cent. or very slightly higher (4 per cent. is the actual minimum demanded by law), so it is obvious that if we take a cucumber, cut it up and put it in a jar, then fill the jar with vinegar, the final strength will be 2 per cent. or lower, for the jar will be more than half cucumber, which is over 95 per cent. water.

Under these conditions fermentation will soon start; white specks will appear indicating infection with wild yeast, and finally moulds will start to grow on top, when our so-called pickles will be thrown into the dust-bin, jar and all!

In commercial pickling this difficulty is overcome by the long processing the vegetables receive. They are brined for weeks and often months; indeed, many of the vegetables used are shipped to England from far countries packed in

2

strong brine, in which they remain till wanted. They are then treated in an acid bath before finally being packed into jars and covered with vinegar. This process removes all fear of fermentation, it also removes most of the flavour, and one is left with a highly acid-cum-salt product that will not stand comparison with a properly prepared home-made pickle.

It is quite simple to get the best of both worlds in domestic pickling, to avoid waste and retain flavour, once we understand what we are trying to do; but before dealing with the process let us examine for a moment our chief ally—vinegar.

There are many kinds of vinegar, but all genuine vinegars are themselves produced by fermentation. Alcohol in various forms is turned into vinegar by the action of an acetic bacterium. Vinegar brewing is a long and highly technical business and incidentally is another illustration of the use of an organism that is a nuisance in other circumstances, for it is this same acetic bacterium which is cultured and trained by the vinegar brewer, that in a wild state turns beer, cider and wine sour when it happens to be able to infect them.

There are many kinds of vinegar, and they usually follow the national drink of the country. In England malt vinegar and spirit vinegar are the most popular, in France and other wine-producing countries wine vinegar is used, whilst in Scotland distilled vinegar holds pride of place— there is no need to point out why!

All genuine vinegars will make pickles, but malt and spirit vinegars are the best owing to their flavour and greater purity. Wine vinegar possesses a delicate flavour that is quite lost in pickles and usually is dearer.

There are two ways in which the necessary acidity may

be got. If ordinary draught vinegar is used, then the vegetables after brining should be packed in their jars and the jars filled with unspiced vinegar. They should be left for forty-eight hours, then the vinegar should be poured off and the jars refilled with the prepared spiced vinegar. If this method is followed, spirit vinegar is even better for the first bath.

The disadvantages are that it takes double the quantity of vinegar and double the time, two important considerations for the modern housewife, but is probably the best method if pickles are wanted for really long storage.

Far simpler is it to use a bottled vinegar of any well-known make. Bottled vinegars are usually of higher strength than draught vinegar, varying between 5 and 6 per cent., and this strength should, after proper brining, give us the correct acidity in the finished pickle. A 6 per cent. vinegar is the ideal for pickling, but though most brewers can supply this, usually it has to be ordered.

Second only in importance as a partner is salt. We have seen that in commercial pickling the vegetables may be in brine for months, but in domestic pickles this is not only unnecessary but undesirable. With one or two exceptions (which will be noted in the actual recipes), brining should be for twenty-four hours only. If the vegetables are prepared one afternoon they can be finished off the next. There are two ways of brining. Dry brining is done by slicing the vegetables, laying them in a dish and sprinkling each layer with salt. This will give a strong brining and may make the finished pickle too salt for some palates, so when the dry-salt method is used the intermediate vinegar bath mentioned above should be given. The other way is to mix a brine of half a pound of salt to three pints of water and use in the proportion of a pint to a pound of vegetables, and for convenience this strength will be referred to throughout the recipes as "standard brine."

Many old cookery books state that the brine should be strong enough to float an egg, but this is rather a chancy method, for the strength will depend on the age of the egg—always a doubtful problem !

The objects of brining are twofold. Salt has a great affinity for water; one knows how moist it will get if kept anywhere damp, and so it extracts some of the water from the vegetables, salt taking its place. That is, the whole mass becomes uniform. But it has another important function. During brining what is known as leaching takes place, and certain constituents of the vegetables are drawn out which would tend to make the finished pickle look cloudy, whilst odd bits and pieces, especially with cauliflower, are rubbed off. All of which makes for a better-looking pickle.

In addition to vinegar and salt we have a third line of defence from spices. Originating in the tropics—hence the famed Spice Isles which are the Moluccas—spices were first used to hide the flavour of half-putrid meats, for in hot climates meat starts to decay almost from the moment it is killed. In the Middle Ages a flourishing trade was done importing them to Europe, as beside the variety of flavourings they can give it was soon found they actually helped to preserve food.

This is because the pungent taste of the different berries, roots, barks, etc., is due to what is called an essential oil, and we now know that these oils possess a strong bactericidal action, though it varies with different spices.

Spices need treating with respect. Many a good pickle has been spoilt by a too lavish hand with clove or

Vinegar usually follows the National Drink of the Country.

cinnamon, but by using common sense an unlimited variety of flavours can be obtained.

There is one rule that should always be observed, never buy ready-mixed spice. Buy the spices separately and mix them yourself in the proportions you require. Of many samples of mixed spice bought at different shops and analysed, no two were found to be the same. Some were preponderant in cloves or ginger, others in mustard or pepper, whilst one or two were quite obviously the dust and debris from the bottom of the tins.

The following list of spices and herbs used in pickling may be of interest.

SPICES AND HERBS

Allspice.—A native of Jamaica. The berry gets its name from the flavour, which seems to be a compound of many other flavours.

Bay Leaves.—The leaves of a small laurel. A native of the Mediterranean. These were the leaves with which the ancient Greeks crowned their heroes.

Cardamom.—The dried fruit of an Indian shrub. There are a number of kinds.

Cayenne Pepper.—Powdered chillies. Named after Cayenne in South America.

Chilli.—The dried seed-pods of Capsicum, an American genus of tropical plants. There are many kinds.

Cinnamon.—The bark of a small tree from Ceylon. The bark is peeled off and dried in the sun, when it curls up into the form we know. **Cassia** is from another tree of the same genus.

Cloves.—The dried flower-buds of the clove tree. The buds are picked when about to open and dried in the sun. About one-fifth their weight is oil of cloves.

Coriander.—An annual plant that flourishes in Asia, America and South Europe. The plant itself has a very disagreeable smell, but the fruit when dried gives the pleasant scent for which it is cultivated.

Ginger.—The root of an East Indian plant. When the plant withers the roots are scalded and dried. Black ginger is unscraped and white ginger scraped.

Mace.—The aril or dried outer layer of the nutmeg fruit.

Mustard.—There are two varieties : the black, brown and red mustards in which the seeds are ground and used whole in pickling, and white mustard which is eaten as a salad in the form of mustard and cress.

Pepper.—A native of India, pepper was once such a luxury that taxes were paid with it. Black pepper is the fruit picked before it is fully ripe and dried. White pepper comes from either the ripe fruit or the coatings of the dried black pepper berry.

Pimento.—Another name for Allspice.

Turmeric.—The root of an East Indian plant which, when dried and ground, gives a yellow powder. This is the base of Curry and Piccalilli.

Herbs are not used as much as the spices, but they can be well utilised to give variety to Chutneys and Sweet Pickles. Many that were familiar to our forefathers (or rather mothers) have fallen out of favour, and many had high repute in medical treatment not so many years ago. Culpeppers' *Herbal*, published in the middle of the seventeenth century, contains many extraordinary recommendations for using herbs to cure all manner of diseases.

The more common ones that are still available include Basil, Borage, Chervil, Chives, Clary, Cummin, Fennel, Garlic, Horehound, Horseradish, Hyssop, Marigold, Marjorum, Mint, Rosemary, Rue, Sage, Samphire, Savory, Shallot, Tarragon, Thyme, Sorrel.

Of these Garlic, Horseradish, Mint, Sage, Shallots, Tarragon and Thyme are the most important for the pickler.

And so having now some idea of the principles of pickling and a nodding acquaintance with the materials we shall use, we must next consider the equally important subject of the process.

Do not gather just after twenty-four hours' rain.

CHAPTER III

THE PROCESS

" Thou shalt be whipp'd with wire and stewed in brine
Smarting in lingering pickle."

Antony and Cleopatra, Act II. Sc. v.

A BAD workman blames his tools, but few housewives would think of blaming their saucepan for bad pickles, yet the utensils are of the greatest importance.

Metal pots and pans of copper, brass or iron must be avoided. Copper and brass are dangerous, whilst iron will turn the pickles black as well as giving a bitter flavour.

Good quality enamel is satisfactory, but it must not be cracked or the vinegar will attack the metal underneath and the enamel will then flake off.

Stainless steel, that latest addition to kitchenware, is the best material of all, and it is from this that most modern factory plant is made; unfortunately, it is still rather expensive.

An alternative is to take the largest round stewpan or saucepan you have—it doesn't matter what it is made of—and buy an ordinary pudding-basin with a rim that will just fit into the pan so that the rim of the basin rests on the edge of the pan, half fill the pan with water and so use the basin as a steamer.

This is in effect the steam-jacketed pan used in commercial pickling, and a plate placed on top makes an effective lid. You cannot do such large quantities at once, but for chutneys and spiced vinegar in limited amounts it is simple and effective, and what is made will be free from any risk of burning or of metallic contamination.

Whilst we are on the subject of cooking there is one simple rule to remember, though like all rules there are times when it has to be broken.

Ordinary sharp pickles should always be made cold. Sweet pickles and spiced fruits need heating but NOT cooking. Chutneys must be properly cooked.

This is because sharp pickles should be crisp and firm; if heated this quality will be lost, and a spongy pickled onion is a thing of horror.

Sweet pickles are mostly fruits put down in a syrup of vinegar and sugar, and need heating through or the syrup will not penetrate the fruit.

Chutneys being a combination of a dozen or more flavours need thoroughly cooking and mixing so that no one flavour predominates.

Many sweet pickles and chutneys can be cooked in their jars, it depends on just how much boiling down the syrup or chutney requires to reach the correct consistency, but advice on this is given in the actual recipes.

Almost any sort of jar is suitable for bottling pickles, provided it has a large enough top to get the vegetables in and out without breaking them and can be made air-tight. Special jars with glass or screw tops can be bought, but if they have any metal parts they are of doubtful suitability as the vinegar may attack the metal.

Ordinary jam-jars are as good as anything, only do see that they are clean, and avoid like the plague any jar that some male member of your family has used for his paint-brushes. Turpentine and paraffin possess most persistent odours which need a great deal of scouring to eliminate.

Hot water, soda and soap, with a thorough final rinse under a cold tap, is all that is necessary for jam-jars that have been stored for some months, though a useful pre-caution is to let them stand full of water after washing, adding to the water a few drops of potassium permanganate solution to colour it a deep pink.

After the final rinse, stand them upside down on a piece of clean newspaper to drain, but don't wipe them dry inside, for this may do more harm than good by spread-ing to all, any possible mould spores there may be in one.

For closing the jars after filling, a double layer of grease-proof paper tied tightly or the cellophane tops that can be bought at any stationer's are quite satisfactory. Don't use corks unless you cover the underside with grease-proof paper, for corks are often full of mould and in commercial practice are well sterilized before use, whilst closing pickle-jars with corks that have been used before is asking for trouble.

For the brining of vegetables, any vessel is suitable except iron, brass or copper. Salt is a comparatively inert substance, and enamel basins, earthenware bread-pans and aluminium pots may be utilized with safety. Only re-member that if you are brining with dry salt, place the vegetables in a deep dish. If you lay onions on a flat one and sprinkle them with salt you will discover a flood the next morning from the water that has been extracted.

For sharp pickles which are prepared without heating, the spiced vinegar must be made beforehand or bought ready spiced. This latter is the simplest, and most vinegar brewers sell good spiced vinegar; but if you are ambitious and industrious enough to make your own and so get that variety of flavour that will give individuality to your pickles, there are two methods.

The first is to soak the spices in cold vinegar for some time before using. This means thinking ahead, and possibly in March you will have other things to worry about than the shallots your husband will pull in June, but it makes the best spiced vinegar. It should be prepared by putting the mixed spice into bottles, about a quarter full, and filling with vinegar, occasionally shaking the bottles but allowing it to settle for some days before use and then decanting the vinegar off. The bottles can then be refilled with vinegar, though after each refilling the spicing will gradually get weaker.

The second way is to add the spices to the vinegar and bring to the boil, and for this it is not necessary to use all the vinegar you require.

Make a concentrated essence in a quart of vinegar, and add this to the bulk. It is not as good as a cold soak-ing and should be done on a morning when everybody else is out of the house, for the smell of hot, spiced vinegar will permeate the whole place.

The following are three typical recipes for spicing vinegar, but one should use imagination and vary the ingredients according to one's own taste. If you hate cloves don't use them—the list in a previous chapter gives plenty of alternatives.

SPICE RECIPES

To be prepared in one quart of 5 per cent. (bottled) vinegar. All spices to be whole and not ground or bruised.

General Mixed Spice	Aromatic Mixed Spice	Hot Mixed Spice
½ oz. cloves.	½ oz. allspice.	1 oz. mustard seed.
½ oz. allspice.	½ oz. coriander.	¼ oz. chillies.
½ oz. cinnamon	¼ oz. cardamom.	½ oz. cloves.
½ oz. ginger.	12 cloves.	½ oz. black pepper.
½ oz. white pepper.	¼ oz. cinnamon.	1 oz. allspice.
	6 bay leaves.	

Spices vary enormously in pungency not only from the quality of the crop but also by the length of time they have been in stock, and so it cannot be too strongly emphasized that one's own discretion is the chief guide to the quantity of each used.

One final note on spices. Cloves, allspice and black pepper should not be used where a white appearance is desired, such as in small white onions or cauliflower, for these spices are apt to stain vegetables, especially where the ends are cut, and though this does not matter where chutneys

If you hate cloves, don't use them.

and piccalillies are concerned, or when there is natural colouring as in red cabbage, it will spoil the look of such pickles as cocktail onions. Incidentally the tendency to staining by spices is not so likely when the spiced vinegar has been prepared cold.

Pickling is the process of preserving good sound vegetables and not a method of using half-decayed stuff; therefore see that your materials are gathered on a dry, mild day and not just after twenty-four hours' rain or when they are full of frost. Then use them at once, don't let them lie on the larder floor for three or four days. It is better to buy a few cucumbers and onions rather than let your beautiful cauliflowers wither because you've nothing else to pickle with them at the moment.

In trimming and cutting never use an ordinary steel knife; that rather rusty old one in the kitchen drawer may be very much sharper, but the ends of the vegetables will stain if you use it, because iron, and tannin which is present in the spices, form ink. Silver or stainless steel knives are admissible, and wooden spoons which can be well scalded before and after use.

Most pickling recipes start off with the admonition: Thoroughly wash the vegetables! Why? When the whole process of pickling is the removal of surplus water, what object is there in adding to it? This is one of those myths that have been handed down from one cookery book to another and is quite unnecessary unless the vegetables are actually dirty, and in that case they are probably not fit to pickle anyway. This does not, of course, apply to the roots where any soil clinging must be washed off, but to such vegetables as cabbage and cauliflower.

Before starting on your process see that everything is ready. Collect the utensils, have the jars washed and the

spiced vinegar made, and then having started, finish the job.
If you brine your materials to-day, intending to pickle them
to-morrow but later decide to finish the day after because
there's a tennis party or what-not on, they'll be too salt,
but by the time you find this out you'll have quite forgotten
why.

One last word, don't waste good stuff. A great deal of
vegetable that would be discarded in cooking is excellent
for pickling, and there is no need to peel a red cabbage to
half its normal size before you start pickling it. On this
we cannot end better than by quoting from the introduction
to *Domestic Cookery Made Easy*, by Hannah Glasse :

" I have heard of a cook that used six pounds of butter
to fry twelve eggs."

Washing is quite unnecessary.

CHAPTER IV

WHAT TO GROW

" First, catch your hare."
Old Recipe for Jugged Hare.

IF you are a keen gardener, always have ample supplies of
fresh vegetables and thoroughly understand their cultivation, this chapter does not concern you.

Yet though primarily this is a book on pickling and
not gardening, a few hints on what to grow cannot be out
of place, and may be of use to the uninitiated, for it will
not be much good wanting to pickle shallots in July unless
you have planted them in the previous February.

The chief vegetables, and those easily and quickly
grown that are used in pickling are cabbage, cucumber,
cauliflower, beetroot, onions and shallots and tomatoes.
As second favourites there are carrots, French beans,
artichokes, radishes, marrow and celery. The fruits come
under a different category as they cannot be produced to
order at short notice, whilst planting a walnut tree in the
hope that you'll ever pickle the produce is just waste of
time or taking a very long view.

But the ordinary vegetables mentioned above can be
grown quickly and economically, and everybody who has a

garden or allotment should allocate some space for pickling vegetables.

In practice this is quite easy, for it only means putting in a few more plants than would normally be needed. Half a dozen red-cabbage plants added to the cabbage patch every time you plant out will provide the material for a constant supply of pickled cabbage, whilst it is not necessary to have a greenhouse or even frames to grow all the tomatoes and cucumbers you want for pickling. Indeed, in the case of these two vegetables the outdoor varieties are definitely better than the more luscious forced type, as they are smaller with firmer flesh and not so liable to go soft when pickled; moreover, the flavour is more pronounced.

The vegetables are in alphabetical order for easy reference and not in importance.

ARTICHOKE. It is the humble " Jerusalems " and not the lordly Globe artichoke that is used for pickling. They have roots rather like potatoes and stems and leaves similar to sunflowers. Actually the Jerusalem artichoke is a close relative of the sunflower. Planting time is from November to February and the tubers are planted four inches deep and eighteen inches apart. If you plant more than one row, leave a space two feet six inches between the rows.

You need not bother overmuch about preparing the ground, a good deep digging is all that is necessary. Most people relegate their artichokes to some odd corner of the garden where the foliage makes a good screen. Artichokes are apt to be very knobbly, but you can succeed in getting them comparatively round and smooth-surfaced if you select only such for planting. Many gardeners dig them up as they are needed and leave the rest in the ground for next year's crop. This is a mistake, as the tubers then become ugly in shape and smaller. Dig the entire crop, therefore, each autumn, and plant fresh tubers every year.

BEETROOT. There are two kinds of beet, the round and the long. The long is usually grown for storage during the winter and the round for use in salads in summer and early autumn.

Grow the round for pickling, as it is quicker growing, more convenient in size, takes up less room and is sweeter and better flavoured. Any date between March and early May is suitable for seeding, but the earlier you sow the sooner will you get the crop—many people make three or four sowings at intervals of three weeks. They are ready for use when the beets are the size of tennis balls, and left long after reaching maturity they become tough and woody.

Beetroot likes a sunny piece of ground where the soil is rich but has NOT been recently manured. Freshly manured ground makes the roots forked and ugly in shape.

The ideal way to sow is to put in groups of three seeds every four inches in a row. If several plants come up (you can expect even half a dozen) at each station, pull all but the strongest. The seeds should be covered one inch deep with soil and, if more than one row, leave nine inches between the rows.

CABBAGE. You may not think it worth while raising your own red-cabbage plants, for any nurseryman will provide a handful for a few pence or if you have a friend with a large garden you can always " borrow " some ! If you want to be independent and raise your own plants, then sow in March or April and your crop will be ready six or seven months later. When the seedlings are showing well but before they appear overcrowded, dig them up carefully so as to avoid root damage, and set them out six inches apart in rows one foot apart on any spare piece of ground. As soon as they are growing strongly, again transplant them once more to their permanent home, which must be rich, sunny soil where they can mature. In this final transplanting set them eighteen inches apart in rows two feet wide.

3

CAULIFLOWER. These are grown in almost the same way as red cabbage, the only difference being that the seeding is done in April and May, with the crop ready for use in the autumn. Cauliflower belongs to the cabbage family and requires the same treatment.

CELERY. Unless you have a greenhouse it is not worth while trying to raise your own celery plants. They require raising under heat and as they are very liable to disease, sterilized mould is necessary in the seed-boxes, so it is far easier to buy strong plants from a nurseryman. Celery must be grown in trenches which are prepared in winter.

They should be dug eighteen inches wide and two feet deep. As you dig throw the top soil on one side and the bottom soil on the other. Enrich the bottom soil by mixing strawy manure with it and then return it to the trench. Then mix some well-rotted manure with the top soil and return half of that to the trench, which will then be filled to within three inches of the top. The surplus top soil is left in a neat ridge beside the trench. Let the trench rest until planting time, which is late May, then prepare the trench by firmly treading and raking. Set out the plants in a double row thus : : : : : : nine inches between each row, and see no crumbs of soil are between the leaves, as this causes rotting and discoloration. Right from the start syringe the plants once a week with soot water to deter their great enemy, the celery fly.

At the beginning of August start earthing up the plants. Take a little soil from the reserve bank and whilst holding the leaves firmly together (or slipping an elastic band over them or tying them with raffia) bank up to a height of four inches in the form of a ridge. See the soil is fine and crumbly, not lumpy. Continue earthing up until they are fully grown. The usual plan is to add four inches of soil every fortnight.

CUCUMBER. You don't need a greenhouse or even a frame to grow cucumbers, for the type known as the " Ridge " is the best for pickling. They are smaller and more fully flavoured. Choose a sunny position well sheltered from the north and east and dig holes two feet deep by two feet square. Put into each two good spadefuls of rotted manure and on top of this four inches of rich soil. In the centre of each station make a twelve-inch-wide and six-inch-high mound of potting mould and in the centre of each mound sow two seeds half an inch deep and two inches apart. The seedlings will soon appear, and when you see which is the stronger, pull out the weaker.

The best time to sow is mid-May, but as it is often a little cold at night you can help the young plants by covering each pair of seeds with an inverted jam-jar, letting it remain until they are growing strongly, but admitting air by tilting it with a stone.

Ridge cucumbers, like the hothouse type, require plenty of moisture, so water freely and syringe every fine evening. The only training they need is to nip off the growing points when the sixth or seventh leaf is formed, and you will find that fruits are born in abundance.

FRENCH BEANS. French beans are the dwarf beans that need no sticks. They are planted in April, May, June or July, or in each of these months if you want continuous crops. Choose a sunny position well away from trees where the soil has been dug and given some manure or fertilizer during the winter.

Dig a flat-bottomed trench two inches deep and nine inches wide and in this set the seeds six inches apart, thus—

. . . . . .

Cover the seeds with fine soil, after which there is nothing much to do, except giving an occasional watering if the weather is dry, until the plants are in flower. Then help the flowers to set into beans by nipping off the long shoots that are trying to emulate their brothers, the runner beans, by shooting into the air. An occasional syringing on hot summer evenings is of assistance in flower-setting.

MARROW. Marrow probably conjures to your mind plants which ramble untidily for yards and yards, entirely clothing the rubbish-heap on which they are growing. Anyone with limited space should never attempt to grow this old type of marrow.

But the " Bush Marrow " makes a compact growth, doesn't ramble and doesn't even need a rubbish-heap on which to grow, whilst it gives just as many fruits as the old kind, and of better quality.

Choosing a sunny, sheltered position, prepare as many stations as you require in the same way as for ridge cucumbers. Dig the pits two feet deep and two parts fill them with manure, rotting garden rubbish, leaf mould, etc., and place on top five inches of garden soil with, in the centre, a further mound six inches wide and six inches deep of potting mould.

Get these stations ready in time to do the sowing in May, and plant one seed in the centre of each mound, protecting it with an inverted jam-jar as for cucumbers.

The training of marrows consists in nipping off the growing point when it has made several strong, broad leaves, and also nipping off the point of each side-shoot after its seventh leaf has appeared.

When the marrow flowers blossom you will notice they are of two kinds, one having a little marrow behind it and the other being a plain flower. The sole purpose of the latter is to fertilize the fruit-carrying flower, and unless this fertilization takes place the little marrow will wither and die.

Normally this is done by bees and insects, but at the time when marrows are in flower there are many other attractions for all the things that fly and crawl, so you can help by plucking off the plain flower, stripping the petals and thrusting the pollen-coated stem into the centre of the fruit-carrying flowers, leaving them there till they drop out of their own accord.

Marrows need plenty of water, indeed it is almost impossible to overdo watering for this plant.

At first trace of brown at tops, bend over to the ground.

ONIONS. If you grow onions in the ordinary way then you can select your picklers from the bulbs that are too small to store. It is better, however, to grow some specially for pickling, and the type to use is the " Silverskin."

Cultivation in either case is the same. Choose a sunny spot where the ground has been deeply dug and manured during the winter, and sow the seed on the first fine day in late February. Sow in rows one foot apart and cover half an inch deep. Sow as thinly as you can, aiming to have the seed well spaced out. Even then you will find the seedlings cluster together. Don't worry about that, onion seedlings are delicious in salads even before the little bulbs start to form, and by drawing on the seedlings for salad purposes you will gradually thin out the rows. The plants should be nine inches apart from the final thinning.

The signal to lift onions is when the foliage is beginning to turn brown at the tips, and at the first trace of this bend the tops over to the ground. This helps the bulbs to ripen properly.

RADISH. There can scarcely be an amateur gardener who has not grown radishes, but few ever pickle them, for it is not the root which is pickled, but the seed-pods. Sow radishes in rich soil that lies rather damp, and instead of only one or two sowings make a dozen or more. A thimbleful of seed every fortnight from March to September is a good plan. This will provide a constant supply of crisp radishes for the table. For pickling, however, they must be allowed to run to seed, and to do this leave a few odd plants in some spot where they won't be a nuisance until they shoot up and flower. Pick the pods before they are fully ripe.

SHALLOTS. The shallot is an onion, but instead of being grown from seed it is planted as a bulb. Planting is done by scooping out a little depression in the soil with a trowel and screwing a bulb into each, the tip of the bulb just projecting above the soil. In July the foliage will begin to turn brown and that is the time to dig the crop. The bulbs need a fortnight lying in the sun before they are properly dried, but don't break up the clusters until drying is completed.

TOMATOES. Never try to raise your own tomato plants from seed, for apart from having to be raised in heat they are most difficult things to rear, and the amateur nearly always fails with them. Nicely grown plants are easily bought at from threepence to sixpence each.

You can grow them in a greenhouse if you have one, but you'll get just as good a crop with much less trouble outdoors. The ideal position is at the foot of a south-facing sunny fence or wall—the back of a flower-border will do—but the soil must be good and well dug and manured.

Plant in May, and as you plant give each tomato a four-foot cane to which it can be loosely tied as it grows. Leaving a little depression in the soil round the stem helps watering.

Soon after planting you will find the plants are beginning to produce side-shoots. This will continue throughout growth and is a nuisance, because side-shoots are definitely not wanted. As each appear it must be nipped off. Leave them and you'll have little or no fruit. The only other attention they need, apart from watering, is pollination. When the flowers begin to appear, borrow a camel-hair brush from your son-and-heir's paint-box and brush lightly from flower to flower. This will mingle the pollen and ensure better fruit-setting.

From those brief notes you should be able to select something to grow on even the tiniest plot of ground, and it is surprising what the odd, neglected corner can produce in the way of food when the right thing is planted.

Remember always, the food you grow yourself tastes so much better !

If you gather them yourself, be certain they are Mushrooms.

CHAPTER V

RECIPES

" The proof of the pickle is in the eating."
Adapted Proverb.

MOST fruits and vegetables can be pickled in some form and the number of recipes is legion, but for those who have had little or no experience of home pickling, a list of the materials normally available may be of assistance.

Apples.—Used chiefly in mixed pickles and chutneys where apples are a useful substitute for the Indian mango. Also spiced whole or with chopped onion as a cheap cottage pickle.

Apricots.—A delicious sweet pickle.

Artichokes.—Popular years ago, but require some cooking.

Asparagus.—Requires cooking before pickling and will probably be eaten then. Rather a waste to pickle.

Bananas.—Makes a good chutney for those who like the taste, but mushy.

Barberries.—An old English sweet pickle given by Mrs. Glasse.

Beans.—Only the French beans are pickled. Best in mixed pickle and chow-chow.

Beetroot.—Usually pickled for immediate use. A rather difficult pickle to keep for any length of time.

Blackberries.—Are best spiced or mixed with other sweet pickle.

Cabbage.—One of the most popular and easy pickles to make. Only the red cabbage is pickled in vinegar, though the green cabbage is used in chow-chow. Sauerkraut is green cabbage pickled in salt.

Carrots.—Not very exciting as a pickle, but the colour is useful mixed with other vegetables.

Cauliflower.—Almost essential in all mixed pickles, piccalillies and chow-chows. Rather insipid alone.

Celery.—An excellent addition to mixed pickles and chow-chow.

Cherries.—Sweet pickled cherries are a delicacy and some should always be made when there is a plentiful crop.

Cranberry.—Makes a good chutney for turkey or game, but cranberries are never plentiful in this country.

Cucumber.—Large ones are best sliced with other vegetables in mixed pickles. The small immature cucumbers are pickled whole as gherkins.

Currants.—Dried currants, not the red, black or white garden currants, are used in chutneys.

Damsons.—Another delightful pickle, especially with cold ham.

Dates.—Though not a home crop they are extensively used in commercial chutneys and sauces.

Elderberry.—Elderberry shoots were much used years ago in place of bamboo shoots. This was when curry first became popular and people were trying to copy the Indian pickles or chutneys as they later were called. The berries also make a chutney.

Fennel.—Probably unheard of to-day, though Mrs. Glasse gives a recipe.

Figs.—Like dates, dried figs are used in commercial sauce and chutney. Green figs make a good sweet pickle, but if you have a fig tree which bears, you'll probably prefer to eat them.

Gooseberries.—They can be spiced whole but are best as a chutney, in which form they are one of the most popular and easy pickles to make.

Grapes.—The small green grapes so often found on old cottages make a good sweet pickle and are widely used on the Continent.

Horseradish.—As this is a root obtainable all the year there is not much object in pickling it, but a little added to mixed pickles gives variety to the flavour.

Lemons.—The taste for pickled lemons has died out, but they make quite an interesting chutney.

Limes.—Mrs. Glasse brackets limes and " stertion seeds " and her recipe is for the berries from the linden and not the tropical lime that gives lime juice.

Marrow.—Properly pickled is good and can be used in mixed pickles and chutneys. Should be used more as it absorbs spice flavours well.

Melon.—A popular vegetable for pickling in America, but is not much grown here owing to the vagaries of the English climate.

Mushrooms.—Probably make the best ketchup of all. Can also be pickled satisfactorily, but if you gather them yourself be certain they are mushrooms, and not the Deathcap (*Amanita phalloides*) or the Fly Agaric (*Amanita muscaria*), both of which are poisonous. If you don't know, don't risk it.

Nasturtiums.—Pickled nasturtium seeds make a good substitute for capers or added to mixed pickles. They should be used more and are simple to do.

Nectarines.—Can be delicious pickled—but why gild the lily? From our tree they never last long enough to have any over for pickling.

Onions.—The most popular pickle of all and a necessity in chutneys and mixed pickles.

Peaches.—The queen of all sweet pickles, whilst dried peaches give a good chutney.

Plums.—Plums are so often very cheap that even if you don't grow them they pay to pickle. Spiced or as a chutney or mixed with apple.

Quince.—Another fruit whose popularity has waned. Its delicate flavour comes out well as a pickle or in chutney.

Radishes.—Mrs. Glasse gives a recipe for pickling radish pods, but they are seldom grown for this purpose to-day.

Raisins and Sultanas.—Though not indigenous to this country, raisins and sultanas must be included owing to the large part they play in chutneys. Both are forms of dried grape imported from the countries bordering the Mediterranean, and this also applies to currants. All kinds are very rich in sugar.

Raspberries.—These are best known in raspberry vinegar, which is excellent and much too little made.

Rhubarb.—Both as a chutney and as a spiced pickle rhubarb is a cheap and good material, and as it grows all the summer it can be utilized for these lcng after its stewing and pie-days are over.

Samphire.—A wild seashore plant, it is gathered in the spring for pickling and is really fine. I have often eaten it in Lincolnshire, and all who live near the seacoast and can obtain it, should pickle some.

Shallot.—Is an onion and plays the same part in pickling.

Tomatoes.—Ubiquitous as a commercial sauce, tomatoes are best pickled green and made as a chutney, though the ripe ones can also be used. Tomatoes mix well with other things, and apples, onions, celery, etc., can all join partnership.

Walnuts.—With the possible exception of a pickled peach nothing can touch a good pickled walnut, either sweet or sharp. But they must be gathered at the right moment, when the fruit is formed but not the shell. This is early in July.

From that list and what you learnt in the previous chapter on " What to Grow " you should have no difficulty in getting all the produce to make a variety of pickles, spiced fruits and chutneys, for Nature always compensates, and if it's a bad year for gooseberries or cherries, then plums and apples will probably be given away.

The recipes have been selected from a collection of over five hundred, and I should like to thank the many people who during a number of years have sent me copies of long-cherished family recipes. They have all been tried out, with almost monotonous satisfaction, and I hope that in giving them wider publicity I shall not be violating some family tradition. After all, a pleasure shared is greater for the sharing, which applies to pickles as to anything else.

The recipes are divided into three groups:

(1) Simple and Mixed Pickles;
(2) Spiced and Pickled Fruits;
(3) Chutneys and Ketchups;

with short Preliminary Notes to each Section.

Peach—the queen of all sweet pickles.

Section One

SIMPLE AND MIXED PICKLES

SIMPLE AND MIXED PICKLES

VEGETABLES and not fruits are the chief materials used, though apples are sometimes included in mixed pickles. Brining for twenty-four hours is generally desirable, and pickling should be done cold, though in the case of the roots some cooking is necessary.

Jars should not be crammed too full of vegetables, and there must be at least an inch of clear vinegar on top which should reach to within an inch of the top of the jar. See the closure is airtight, and after tying down, store in a cool, dry place free from draught.

If, on examination after a few days, the vinegar is evaporating, the jar is either not airtight or the storage too warm. The jars should be filled up and moved.

Simple pickles are not fit to eat for some two weeks, with the exception of the cooked roots, and are in their prime in a couple of months. Thereafter they tend to soften, so too long maturing is not desirable. In all cases soak in the final spiced vinegar for twenty-four hours, if possible, before packing into jars. This allows the vinegar to penetrate much better than after packing.

ARTICHOKES

Of the two kinds of artichoke, Globe and Jerusalem, the latter makes the best pickle but, like all roots, it does not keep too well, and requires cooking.

Clean and peel the tubers and boil for about ten minutes in half-strength brine, *i.e.* a quarter of a pound of salt to six pints of water. Artichokes have a delicate flavour which too strong brining will spoil. Don't let them get soft or they fall to pieces in the pickle.

Drain until cold, pack into wide-mouthed jars, and cover with spiced vinegar, preferably hot spice, and if you add some shredded horseradish they go well with cold beef.

ASPARAGUS

If you possess a large asparagus-bed and have more grass than you can eat, then it is well worth while pickling a few jars.

Take large heads and cut only as far as it is green, place these loosely in a standard brine and simmer for five minutes. Drain and pack into jars (they should be packed in single layers so that with each layer the heads face differently). Cover with unspiced vinegar just on the boil and stand for a week. Drain off this vinegar and re-cover with boiling spiced vinegar, using a general mixed spice.

Tie tightly and they will be fit in two weeks; but small jars should be used, so that once opened they are soon eaten.

BEANS

The french bean is an annoying vine in that the pods mature so quickly once they really start. One is therefore likely to have surplus beans at a time of year when there are masses of other stuff.

They may be pickled in plain salt for use as a vegetable later, in the same way that Sauerkraut is made. For this select small pods and pack in layers of salt and beans, allowing a quarter-pound of salt to each pound of beans. This is not counting a layer of salt at the bottom and a final layer on top. After a few days they will have shrunk and the jar should be filled up again. If it is a large jar, this may need doing two or three times.

When finally full, make thoroughly airtight.

For use they require de-salting by soaking in cold water for twenty-four hours, adding about half a teacupful of vinegar to the water—just enough to make it taste—and changing the water three or four times. Then cook in the ordinary way.

As a pickle they are best in piccalilli or chow-chow, though *Domestic Cookery* gives a recipe for pickling them which requires covering with boiling vinegar every twenty-four hours for five days. It's not worth it.

If, however, you want to pickle some for use in mixed pickles or chow-chow later, give a twenty-four-hour brine, pack into jars and cover with unspiced vinegar. In a few weeks when other vegetables are ready, you can mix them in.

BEETROOT

Beetroots are obtainable most of the year and, like all the root crops, require cooking before pickling. Wash off any soil still clinging to the roots, taking care not to break the skin, for beetroot bleeds easily. If pickling for immediate use, simmer for one and a half to two hours. When cold, skin and cut into squares or slices, and cover with unspiced or spiced vinegar, whichever you prefer.

If pickling for storage, bake the roots in a moderate oven until tender and, when cold, skin and cut into squares—it packs better that way for keeping ; cover with spiced vinegar to which has been added half an ounce of salt to each pint.

Beetroot contains a good deal of sugar, and fermentation is more likely than with other vegetables, so seal thoroughly well to exclude air.

CABBAGE

Red cabbage can be had through most of the year, and as it is a pickle that matures quickly and is fit to eat in a week, it should not be made in too large a quantity at once, as after a couple of months it tends to soften.

Take off the coarse outer leaves and quarter the cabbage, then shred across the grain. Lay in a deep bowl, sprinkling with dry salt, and leave for twenty-four hours, mixing once or twice.

Take out of brine and drain well for an hour, then put back into the bowl and cover with spiced vinegar, either general mixed spice or hot mixed spice, and leave for another twenty-four hours, again mixing occasionally.

Then pack into jars and cover with the vinegar, but don't pack too tightly, for cabbage packs close. A little shredded horseradish in some jars adds variety, whilst in America it is often mixed with finely sliced onion.

4

CARROTS

The natural flavour of carrot is not sufficiently thrilling to make it a popular straight pickle, but the colour is useful for garnishing or mixing with other clear pickles, so a few jars should occasionally be put down.

Select medium-sized carrots, scrape and boil in standard brine until tender but not soft. Drain thoroughly, then cut in circles or lengthwise into strips. It is well to do some of each as the different shapes help in decoration. Pack, not too tightly, into jars and cover with cold unspiced vinegar, let them stand a week, drain off the vinegar and re-cover with cold spiced vinegar. Use whichever spiced vinegar you fancy and tie securely. Carrot adds greatly to the appearance of salads, and for decoration the circles can be cut into stars or squares.

CAULIFLOWER

Cauliflower must not be too mature for pickling and close-packed heads are best. Break into even-sized pieces, but don't use a knife at all (the stalk of cauliflower stains easily and this is less likely to occur when broken and not cut).

Steep in a standard brine for twenty-four hours, drain really well, pack into jars and cover with cold spiced vinegar. If pickling for use later in other mixed pickles, unspiced vinegar can be used for the temporary pickling.

As a straight pickle, cauliflower is best sweet, and this can most easily be done by adding anything from a teaspoonful to a table-spoonful of sugar (according to the size of the jar) a couple of days before the pickle is wanted. Turn the jar up two or three times till the sugar is dissolved. This is much simpler than putting down in a sweet pickle and less likely to develop fermentation.

CUCUMBER

The easiest way to pickle large cucumbers is to quarter them lengthwise, cut into smaller pieces, brine with dry salt for twenty-four hours, then pack and cover with spiced vinegar. Like most of the vegetables they are best mixed with others and are in many of the recipes under Mixed Pickles.

The small immature cucumbers that are known as dills or gherkins require a longer process, especially if their deep green colour is to be fixed, and they need partial cooking.

No. 1.—Select the gherkins of a uniform size, place in a saucepan and cover with standard brine (half a pound salt to three pints water). Bring to nearly boiling-point, only don't actually boil, but simmer for ten minutes.

Drain until cold, then pack into jars and cover with spiced vinegar, preferably aromatic.

No. 2.—Brine the gherkins for three days in standard brine. Drain off the brine and repeat for another three days. Drain and soak in water to which alum has been added in the proportion of one dessertspoonful to two quarts for six hours, then drain well and simmer for ten minutes in spiced vinegar, pack into warmed jars and cover with the still hot vinegar. The first is the simplest, but No. 2 gives rather a better colour.

ELDERBERRY SHOOTS

Elder shoots were used a good deal during the eighteenth century as a substitute for bamboo shoots, as the latter are a striking constituent of genuine Indian chutneys and Chinese chow-chow, both of which had been popularized by the old East India Company with the introduction of curries.

If, therefore, you are interested in the Indian pickle type, a few jars of elder shoots should be put down in the end of April or beginning of May.

Elder abounds in hedgerows and coppices, and the young green shoots should be gathered before the leaves unfold and cut into two-inch pieces.

They need no brining but can be packed into jars and covered with spiced vinegar, either mixed spice or hot, and used later when you are making mixed pickles or chutneys.

Domestic Cookery (1820) also recommends taking the elder flowers just before they open, and they certainly make an interesting pickle not unlike Samphire, but with the characteristic elder flavour. They can be used in place of capers with boiled mutton.

FENNEL

This herb is chiefly associated with fish, and it is still used as a constituent of fish sauce.

Mrs. Glasse gives a recipe for pickling it, and Culpepper is full of its praises and advises it as a cure for all manner of troubles. He says, " The seed boiled in wine and drunk is good for those that are bitten with serpents or have eaten poisonous herbs or mushrooms."

To pickle, tie young fennel into small bunches with cotton and steep in a standard brine which is just simmering. Drain till cold, pack into jars and cover with unspiced vinegar. It can then be taken out a bunch at a time and used for fish sauces and garnishing.

HORSERADISH

Though this root is obtainable more or less always, it is sometimes an advantage to have a few small jars pickled if only to avoid digging it up during inclement weather.

Wash the roots in hot water, scrape off the skin, then either grate or put through a mincer. It needs no brining, but add a teaspoonful of salt to each half-pint of vinegar used. Pack loosely into small jars and cover with the salted vinegar. It can be used straight or mixed with cream and sugar for horseradish sauce.

MARROW

Marrow pickle is like marrow jam, people either love it or loathe it, yet it makes a good pickle though slight cooking is necessary. Many old recipes tell you to " take one marrow," but as it may weigh anything from one to fifteen pounds this is rather vague. Here we are taking five pounds of prepared marrow as the basis.

As it is 95 per cent. water, dry brining is best. Peel the marrow and take out all seeds, then cut lengthwise and chop into small squares and weigh out five pounds. Place this in a deep dish in layers, sprinkling each layer with salt, a quarter of a pound to every two pounds of marrow. Allow it to stand overnight, but twenty-four hours is not needed as the flesh of marrow is so open and it brines easily.

To one quart of spiced vinegar add half a pound of sugar and half an ounce of ground ginger and bring to the boil. Then put in the marrow, which must have been well drained, and cook for ten or fifteen minutes until tender but not soft. Take out of the vinegar and put into warmed jars, then bring the liquor once more to the boil and pour over the marrow. Seal whilst still hot, as this helps to keep it sterile.

MUSHROOMS

Pickled mushrooms were very popular years ago. Mrs. Glasse gives five recipes for preparing them, including one " to keep them twenty years "; but they have since fallen out of favour, probably owing to the publicity given to cases of accidental poisoning. There are over a thousand kinds of fungi found in Britain, many of which are edible, but a few are deadly. The genuine mushroom does not grow under trees or in woods nor in damp, boggy places. Its home is dry, windswept pasture, the flesh is white and the gills pink, turning to brown as they mature. The stem is solid and not hollow, and the gills are not attached to the stem. The top peels easily—but don't rely on this as a test, for so do many other forms. The safest criterion of all is the local villager, to whom the mushroom fields are well known and who has gathered them there for years.

For pickling, mushrooms need no brining. Peel them and put them in layers in a pie-dish, sprinkling each layer with salt, a teaspoonful to each pound of mushrooms. Cover with spiced vinegar and cook in the oven until they are quite tender, then pack into jars and pour the hot liquor on top. Tie down whilst still hot. Pickled this way they keep well and the liquor is a useful ketchup.

NASTURTIUMS

Even the smallest garden boasts nasturtiums, and the seeds when pickled are a good substitute for capers, and can add variety to salad dressings. As a straight pickle they are rather too small to be popular on the table, but go well in clear mixed pickles.

Gather the seeds whilst still green and steep in standard brine for twenty-four hours. Pack into small jars, warm in the oven for ten minutes and cover with hot spiced vinegar. It is best to use a hot spice mixture for these, and a few leaves of tarragon, if available, are pleasing.

The only important thing to remember is to use small jars or bottles, so that they are consumed at once when opened.

ONIONS

Onions are the most popular of all straight pickles, and are the simplest to make. There are countless recipes, some very involved, and three are given. The easiest is the cottage method.

1. *Cottage Recipe.*—Select onions of equal size. Place in hot water and peel, then brine with dry salt—quarter of a pound to every two pounds of onions—in a deep dish and stand for twenty-four hours, stirring up once or twice. Drain, and pack into jars and cover with cold spiced vinegar. They will not be mature for a month and will still be crisp in six months.

2. As before, choose onions of even size, skin and dry them. Take sufficient spiced vinegar to cover (the quantity will vary with the size of the onions) and add half an ounce of salt to each pint. Bring the vinegar to the boil and put in the onions. Simmer for fifteen minutes, pack the onions into warmed jars and cover with the boiling vinegar. In this method they are fit to eat in two days, but go soft more quickly.

3. *American Method.*—Choose small onions, peel and cover with standard brine, and allow to steep two days. Change the brine and stand for two more days, then cover with unspiced vinegar for forty-eight hours.

Drain, and put into jars and cover with spiced vinegar to which has been added a quarter of a pound of sugar to each quart of vinegar. Cover closely and mature.

In all cases the addition of a few whole chillies and whole white pepper aids the appearance, but don't add whole cloves or allspice, or the ends of the onions may stain.

RADISH PODS

The authority for this pickle is Mrs. Glasse, though the trouble involved makes it of doubtful utility to-day. When made, however, it has a very distinctive flavour and goes particularly well in salads.

The seed-pods must be gathered whilst still green and soaked in HOT brine for twenty-four hours. The next day drain, boil up the brine and resoak for a further twenty-four hours. Drain well, pack into jars and cover with hot spiced vinegar, and tie down whilst still hot. The process is very similar to some of the gherkin recipes, and the object of the long treatment is to get them as green as possible.

If preferred, the Glasse recipe can be followed, which means steeping the pods in cold brine for ten days, then packing into jars and covering with hot vinegar, draining off the vinegar twice and reheating after three days' standing.

Personally I eat my radishes raw !

SAMPHIRE

Writing in 1653, Nicholas Culpepper said of samphire : " It was in former times wont to be used more than now it is, the more is the Pity "—a sentiment with which I heartily agree, and so will anyone who has tasted it pickled.

It must be gathered young and green towards the end of July, just before it flowers. Lay in a deep dish in pieces about two inches long, sprinkle with dry salt and stand twenty-four hours.

Drain, then cook slowly till tender in vinegar that just covers it, but be careful not to let it get soft. Pack into jars, pour the vinegar over and tie down. Unspiced vinegar can be used, as the samphire has a distinct peppery flavour which spices only spoil.

SHALLOTS

Shallots are treated like onions, but they are more oval in shape and of firmer texture, and so require longer maturing. Skin the shallots, being careful to cut the ends clean, and brine with dry salt for twenty-four hours. Pack into jars and cover with cold spiced vinegar, and mature for at least two months before using.

If they are wanted for more immediate consumption they can be treated like No. 2 recipe for onions, but even here they need a couple of weeks before they will be ready for use.

TOMATOES

The history of the tomato is a romance, for it is little more than a hundred years since it was first introduced as a table decoration under the name of " Love Apples." Though used so extensively as soup, sauce and chutney, it is rather a disappointment when pickled alone, though it pickles well either ripe or green. Here, however, are two recipes, one for green and one for ripe tomatoes, but you will find the chutneys much more satisfactory.

1. *Green Tomatoes.*—Cut the tomatoes in half and pack into jars with slices of onion. Cover with spiced vinegar to which has been added a teaspoonful of salt to a pint. Place the jar in a slow oven and cook gently for one hour. Tie down whilst still hot.

2. *Ripe Tomatoes.*—Scald the tomatoes and remove the skins. Choose small fruit, as they must not be cut. Place in jars and cover with shallot vinegar, or if you haven't this, boil up in vinegar two sliced onions, remove the onions and pour the vinegar into the jars. Cook in the oven for half an hour and tie down whilst hot.

Owing to the fact that tomatoes are so soft, it is difficult to do them as a straight pickle satisfactorily. They will probably break and you'll end with jars of something that is neither a chutney nor a pickle ; but they can be done, and the ripe ones certainly look nice if they can be got out of the jars whole.

WALNUTS

Only a pickled peach can beat a good pickled walnut, and not always then. Be certain the nuts are not over-ripe, for no amount of pickling will soften the shell once it has formed. Walnuts must be pricked deeply with a silver fork in two or three places. Then soak in a standard brine for at least three days—some recipes give as much as ten days' brining, but so long is not absolutely necessary.

Take them from the brine and place on a tray or cloth in the sun, moving occasionally. Slowly they will turn black. For the average English summer this will take two days, but if it happens to be one of our rare heat-waves, twenty-four hours may suffice.

When quite black, pack into jars and cover with spiced vinegar. Tie down and mature for at least a month before use. That is the simple cottage way of pickling them, but there are many more complicated recipes, some of which are given.

1. Take one hundred walnuts and prick well. Soak in a brine of one and a half breakfast-cupsful of salt to each quart of water for nine days, changing the brine every three days. Drain, and place in the sun until black, then pack into jars. For the vinegar, mix to each quart two ounces of whole black pepper, one ounce of allspice, one ounce of bruised ginger, three shallots and half a pound of brown sugar. Boil these in the vinegar for ten minutes and pour over the nuts, dividing the spices equally in the jars. Cover and seal whilst hot, and store in a cool place. A note to this recipe, which is a private one, says, " They will be fit for use in a month, but will keep two or three years."

2. *Green Pickled Walnuts.*—We are indebted to Mrs. Glasse for this recipe. Her original is very complicated, but simplified it was found quite satisfactory. Choose large walnuts and peel as thinly as possible, throwing each as it is peeled into a standard brine. Allow to steep twenty-four hours, then pack into jars and cover with cold spiced vinegar, but excluding cloves in the spices. Tie down and store for at least three months—longer if your curiosity will allow. Mrs. Glasse says they will keep two

or three years, and certainly some prepared over eighteen months ago are still bright green.

3. *White Pickled Walnuts.*—Again the ubiquitous Mrs. Glasse. Even more complicated in the original, but easily simplified. Choose large nuts and peel until the white flesh appears. Place in standard brine for twelve hours only, and it is important to see the nuts are covered, so place a heavy plate on top or they will blacken.

Transfer to fresh brine and simmer for five minutes, then pack into jars and cover with DISTILLED spiced vinegar, which is white. A few whole chillies and white peppercorns may be added to the jars. Tie down and mature for two months. Be certain the nuts are well covered with vinegar, and store in a dark cupboard.

MIXED PICKLES

Judging by old cookery books the popularity of mixed pickles is comparatively recent. They are not mentioned by Mrs. Glasse, but *Domestic Cookery* gives an interesting recipe for a mixture of apples, cucumber and onions.

The interest lies in the fact that she describes it as " an excellent but NOT COMMON, pickle, called Salade," and this is not to be confounded with " salad " which was well known and popular in many forms. The recipe is so attractive and simple that the quotation is given in full :

" Fill a pint stone jar with equal quantities of onions, cucumbers and sour apples, all cut in very thin slices, shaking in as you go on a teaspoonful of salt and three parts of a teaspoon of cayenne. Pour in a wine-glassful of soy, the same of white wine and fill up the jar with vinegar. It will be fit for use the same day."

A little sugar can take the place of the soy and wine, with a dash of Worcester sauce, and the recipe is as applicable to-day as it was a hundred and thirty years ago.

Most vegetables mix well in pickles, but with the simpler cottage recipes of two things a certain discretion must be shown. For instance, onions and apples are excellent together, but don't try onions and asparagus or cauliflower and beetroot. They don't marry well !

Whenever apples are used they should be sour or cooking apples, the more luscious eating varieties when ripe soften too easily to be satisfactory.

The following are simple cottage recipes of mixtures of two or three things, quickly and easily made :

APPLES AND ONIONS

1 lb. of sour apples.
1 lb. of onions.
1½ to 2 pints of spiced vinegar.
½ oz. of salt.

Peel and core the apples and skin the onions, then slice both, mix well and pack into jars. Add the salt to sufficient vinegar to cover (but this will vary in quantity slightly with the condition of the apples and onions), and fill the jars full. Tie down and store for a week. If wanted for immediate use, heating the vinegar and pouring into the jars hot will make the pickle ready when cold.

CAULIFLOWER, CUCUMBER, FRENCH BEANS, ONIONS AND MARROW

When marrow is being used in mixed pickles it is advisable to brine it separately, so that the cubes retain their shape. Prepare all the other vegetables and steep in a standard brine for twenty-four hours, then drain and cover with unspiced vinegar for twelve hours. At the same time prepare the marrow by peeling, removing all seeds and cutting into small squares about half to one inch thick. Sprinkle with dry salt and allow to stand for twelve hours, then drain well.

Pack the various ingredients into jars and cover with cold spiced vinegar. Two or three weeks' maturing is necessary before they will be fit to eat.

CAULIFLOWER, CUCUMBER AND ONIONS

Another cold mixture in which the quantities of each do not matter, though they should be about equal.

Break the cauliflower head into small pieces, slice the cucumber into various shapes, and peel the onions.

Place all the vegetables in a standard brine of half a pound of salt to three pints of water, allowing a pint to each pound of prepared vegetable. Soak for twenty-four hours, then drain well and cover with unspiced vinegar and allow to stand for a further twenty-four hours.

Pack into jars and cover with spiced vinegar, adding to each jar a few whole chillies.

This is the simplest way of making sharp, mixed pickles, but they will not be ready to eat for two or three weeks, though thereafter will keep for a year.

In many ways the more complicated mixed pickles are the easiest to make. In country villages they still follow the process of filling a large jar three-quarters full of vinegar, putting the vegetables in as they come along; but this is not advisable, as the vegetables become bruised or broken in stirring up to mix them. There is no need, however, for the housewife to be bound by the quantities or type of ingredient given in the following mixtures, and almost anything that is available may be added successfully.

Care should be taken in the packing of the jars, especially if glass jars are used, and in commercial practice great attention is given to this, first an onion, then cauliflower, then cucumber and so on, so that one jar is not all cauliflower and another French beans.

CAULIFLOWER, ONIONS, CUCUMBER AND FRENCH BEANS

Prepare all the vegetables and soak in a standard brine for twenty-four hours. Use about equal quantities of each and as far as possible get them into equal size pieces—this will be governed by the size of your onions. Drain well and pack into the jars adding a thin slice of lemon, a chillie or pickled carrot. Cover with mixed spice vinegar, seal down and store for at least a month before using.

CUCUMBER AND ONIONS

2 lbs. of cucumber.
1 lb. of onions.
1½ pints of spiced vinegar.

Cut the cucumber into small triangles by slicing about half an inch thick, then cutting across. Peel the onions and slice thinly. Mix together, place in a deep bowl and cover with salt—quarter of a pound to every two pounds of prepared vegetable. Brine for twenty-four hours, then drain well. Pack into jars and cover with unspiced vinegar for twenty-four hours, drain and re-cover with spiced vinegar.

Tie down well and mature for two weeks before using. Here again, if wanted more urgently, hot vinegar may be used and the intermediate vinegar-bath ignored, but then the pickle will not keep so well and must be eaten soon. Also it is better to give a wet brine of the standard half-pound of salt to three pints of water, using a pint to a pound of vegetables for this later method, or the finished pickle will be too salt.

GREEN TOMATOES, CABBAGE, CAULIFLOWER, ONIONS, CUCUMBER, CELERY AND FRENCH BEANS

A very mixed brew to which anything else may be added that comes to hand. Cut the tomatoes into quarters, remove the outer leaves of the cabbage (which must be green or white, NOT the red cabbage) and cut into slices about half an inch wide, break up the cauliflower, peel the onions, cut the cucumber, chop the celery into inch pieces and the French beans in half.

Having done all that, put everything except the tomatoes into a standard brine and steep for twenty-four hours. The tomatoes sprinkle with dry salt only.

Drain all and pack neatly into jars, then cover with boiling spiced vinegar, having warmed the jars first or they will crack. In using tomatoes in mixed pickle it is best to have only the one treatment and not to give two vinegar-baths, as the inside fleshy part of tomatoes so easily comes away.

Tie down securely and mature for a month.

All clear mixed pickles may be sweetened if desired, but this is done best a few days before they are required by adding a tablespoonful or so of sugar to each jar, turning up once or twice until the sugar is dissolved. Red and yellow chillies, thin slices of lemon, a few whole spices or a small stick of cinnamon, can be added to the jars for adornment, but be careful that you don't overspice.

MARROW AND ONIONS

Marrow makes a good mixture with small onions, but requires cooking.

> 4 lbs. of prepared marrow.
> 2 lbs. of small onions.
> ¼ lb. of sugar.
> 1 quart of vinegar.

Peel the marrow and cut the flesh into cubes, weigh four pounds, lay in a deep dish in layers, and brine with dry salt, a quarter of a pound to every two pounds of marrow. Stand overnight, then drain well.

Peel the onions, add the sugar to the spiced vinegar and bring to the boil, then put in the onions and simmer for fifteen minutes. Add the marrow and simmer for a further ten minutes, or until just tender, but be careful the marrow does not become too soft. Transfer to hot jars and tie down. A few whole chillies are an addition to the jars for appearance.

RED TOMATOES, CELERY AND ONIONS

A private recipe for an uncooked, simple mixture which is easy to prepare and which keeps well:

3 lbs. of ripe tomatoes.	6 tablespoonsful of mustard seed.
1 lb. of chopped celery.	½ teaspoonful of ground cloves.
½ lb. of chopped onion.	½ teaspoonful of ground cinnamon.
4 tablespoonsful of salt.	1 teaspoonful of grated nutmeg.
6 tablespoonsful of sugar.	1½ pints of unspiced vinegar.

Peel and slice the tomatoes and chop the onions, then mix all the ingredients together in the order given. Pack into stone jars and cover. This uncooked mixture must stand a week before using, but may be kept a year if well sealed.

5

TOMATOES AND ONIONS (Spanish Pickle)

This is a Spanish recipe for using green tomatoes and is similar to many of the green tomato chutneys, but is not so mushy.

7 lbs. of green tomatoes.	$\frac{1}{2}$ oz. of peppercorns.
2 lbs. of onions.	$\frac{1}{2}$ oz. of mustard seed.
$\frac{1}{2}$ lb. of salt.	3 pints of spirit vinegar.
$\frac{1}{2}$ oz. of cloves.	1 lb. of sugar.
$\frac{1}{2}$ oz. of allspice.	

Cut the tomatoes into slices and chop the onion finely. Spread in alternate layers in a deep dish, sprinkling with the salt and mixing in the spices. Stand for twenty-four hours, then drain well. Place in a preserving-pan and cover with the vinegar and sugar, bring to the boil and simmer for half an hour. Fill into warmed jars and tie down. It is ready for use in a couple of days and will keep for some time.

If you don't like whole spices in pickles, they may be boiled in the vinegar for ten minutes first and removed before you put in the tomatoes and onions, but then it is not a true Spanish pickle.

PICCALILLI

There are two kinds of piccalilli. In this country we usually understand the word to mean a sharp, mixed vegetable pickle thickened with mustard and turmeric. In America it means a sweet, clear, mixed pickle, and a recipe for this type is given first.

American Piccalilli

3½ lbs. of green tomatoes.	1 root of horseradish.
½ a large cabbage heart.	2 inches of cinnamon stick.
1 large head of celery.	1 teaspoonful of allspice berries.
2 lbs. of small onions.	1 teaspoonful of cloves.
3 large cucumbers.	2 lbs. of brown sugar.
1 large cauliflower.	2 quarts of vinegar.

Cut the cucumbers, tomatoes, cauliflower and cabbage into small pieces and scrape and slice the celery. Peel the onions and chop fairly fine, then place all in a deep basin and cover with standard brine for twenty-four hours. Tie the spices in a muslin bag and place in the vinegar, bring to the boil, then add the sugar and scraped horseradish.

Simmer for five minutes, then pour into the jars, which have been filled with the drained vegetables.

Seal well and mature for a month.

Other mixtures can be treated in the same way, for strictly speaking this is a sweet mixed pickle in which the sugar is added first.

English Piccalilli

Most housewives who have been used to making pickles have their own recipes for piccalilli, and very good some of them are. The following three samples are quite easy to prepare and keep well.

(1)   2 lbs. of onions.
      2 lbs. of marrow.
      1 large cauliflower.
      1 large cucumber.
      1 lb. of French beans.

Prepare the vegetables by peeling and cutting the marrow, peeling the onions and breaking the cauliflower. Slice the cucumber into half-inch quarters and the beans in half. Place all in a deep bowl and cover with standard brine, and allow to steep for twenty-four hours. Then drain well.

Have ready the following paste :

      1 cup of flour (NOT self-raising).
      $\frac{1}{4}$ lb. of mustard.
      1 oz. of turmeric powder.

Mix together with two quarts of vinegar and boil until it thickens. Then add the vegetables, heat through but do not boil. Fill into warmed jars and tie down well.

(2)   2 lbs. of green tomatoes.
      1 small white cabbage heart.
      1 large or 2 small cucumbers.
      1 lb. of onions.

Prepare and chop all the vegetables into equal sized pieces, including the onions. Place in a deep dish and sprinkle with dry salt, a quarter of a pound to every two pounds of vegetables. Allow to stand twenty-four hours, then drain. Have ready the following pickle :

To one quart of spiced vinegar add one pound of brown sugar and one ounce of turmeric, and bring to the boil.

Take half an ounce of ground mustard and mix it well with two tablespoonsful of olive oil until it is a thick paste. Add this slowly to the hot vinegar and then pour over the vegetables which have been packed into warmed jars. Cover well and mature for two weeks.

> (3) 1 lb. of onions.
> 1 lb. of tomatoes.
> ½ lb. of gherkins.
> 6 chopped shallots.
> 1 large cauliflower.

Prepare the vegetables and chop into small pieces, then place all in a saucepan and cover with standard brine.

Bring to the boil in the brine but don't cook. Drain and allow to cool.

Mix in cold vinegar one ounce of mustard and one teaspoonful of turmeric and add this slowly to one and a half pints of spiced vinegar, and bring to the boil.

Pack the drained chopped vegetables into jars and cover with the hot pickle. Don't pack the jars too tightly; in fact, when making piccalilli this way it is as well to fill the jars with a little vegetable, then pickle, and so on, in order to get an even mixture.

Chow-chow is of Chinese origin and always contains celery.

CHOW-CHOW (I)

Chow-chow is a thick piccalilli of Chinese origin, and its outstanding characteristic is that it always contains celery. The method of preparation is the same as with piccalilli and mustard pickles. Here are two recipes :

(1)   5 lbs. of small green tomatoes.   ¼ lb. of mustard seed.
    12 small cucumbers (gherkins).   2 ozs. of turmeric.
      1 cauliflower.   ½ oz. of allspice.
      2 heads of celery.   ½ oz. of cloves.
      1 pint of small onions.   ½ oz. of pepper.
      2 quarts of string beans.   6 to 8 pints of vinegar.

The quantity of vinegar will vary with the size of the cauliflower and celery heads.

Prepare the vegetables and cut or break all into even-sized pieces. Sprinkle with dry salt and stand for twenty-four hours, then drain.

Mix the spices with the vinegar as for piccalilli, then add the vegetables and cook until tender. Fill into warmed jars.

CHOW-CHOW (2)

(2) 1 lb. of cucumber.	½ lb. of sugar.
1 lb. of onions.	3 ozs. of mustard.
1 lb. of green tomatoes.	2 ozs. of flour.
1 lb. of French beans.	½ oz. of turmeric.
1 lb. of cauliflower.	1 quart of spiced vinegar,
1 lb. of chopped celery.	preferably aromatic, but
1 lb. of shredded cabbage.	certainly not hot spice.

The weights are for prepared vegetables, which should be cut or broken into small pieces. Place in a deep bowl and brine in standard brine for twenty-four hours. Drain well, and cover with unspiced vinegar for twelve hours.

Mix the mustard, sugar, flour and turmeric into a paste, bring the rest of the vinegar to the boil and stir in the paste, then add the vegetables, which must have been drained from the vinegar-bath.

Simmer for twenty minutes, then fill into warmed jars. Owing to the double vinegar pickle this recipe keeps very well.

MUSTARD PICKLES (I)

Like piccalilli, mustard pickle means rather different things in different countries. On the Continent and in parts of America it is a more or less clear pickle of ripe cucumbers heavily spiced with whole mustard seed. Cucumber is seldom ripened in this country, but they can be bought in brine, so here is the recipe.

1. *Mustard Pickle* (Senfgurken).—Peel large yellow cucumbers and remove the seed, then cut into pieces two inches long. Lay in a dish and sprinkle with dry salt, allowing one tablespoonful of salt to each pound of prepared cucumber. Allow to stand twelve hours, then drain well. Pack in layers in two-pound glass jars, mixing in with each jar two ounces of whole mustard seed, one teaspoonful of allspice, one small onion chopped and a little shredded horseradish.

To each quart of spirit or cider vinegar (NOT malt), add six bay leaves and two ounces of sugar.

Boil for five minutes, allow to cool and pour into the jars, placing the bay leaves on top.

Tie securely and store for two weeks before using.

MUSTARD PICKLES (2)

2. *Mustard Pickle* (English).

1 lb. of cucumber.	3 pints of vinegar.
1 lb. of onions.	2 ozs. of sugar.
½ lb. of carrots.	2 ozs. of mustard.
1 cauliflower.	1 oz. of salt.

Prepare the vegetables and chop into even-sized pieces, but keep the carrots and cauliflower separate.

Add the sugar and salt to the vinegar and bring to the boil, then stir in the mustard, slowly, mixed first with a little of the vinegar. Next add the cauliflower and carrot, and boil for fifteen minutes; then add the other vegetables and cook until tender.

Pour into warmed jars and seal down.

3. *Mustard Pickle* (with cabbage). In Canada they make a mustard pickle from green cabbage and onions. It can be very good.

> 2 lbs. of shredded cabbage heart.
> 1 lb. of sliced onion.
> 1 quart of spiced vinegar.
> 1½ ozs. of mustard.
> ½ oz. of turmeric.

Mix the shredded vegetables in a bowl and sprinkle with dry salt, a quarter of a pound to each two pounds of cabbage and onion.

Allow to stand twenty-four hours, then drain.

Mix the mustard and turmeric into a paste with a little vinegar, boil the rest and add the paste to it, stirring till it thickens. Then add the drained vegetables and simmer for ten minutes.

Pack into warmed jars and seal down. Ready to eat in two or three days.

PICKLED AND SPICED
FRUITS

PICKLED AND SPICED FRUITS

FRUIT is far too much neglected in this country, for in America and the Dominions most housewives pickle some at the same time that they make their jams.

This neglect on our part is the more surprising in view of the definite trend in public taste towards sweeter and softer flavoured pickles and sauces, but is probably explained by the fact that, whilst they are easy to do at home, fruit has never been very attractive to the commercial picklers.

Pickled and spiced fruit packs best in proper preserving jars which can be hermetically sealed, it should be sound and un-bruised, and under rather than over ripe. No brining is needed, but care in the heating, as pickled fruit must not be overcooked or it becomes mushy.

In some cases spiced distilled vinegar, cider vinegar or spirit vinegar is preferable, and the spicing should always be on the aromatic side—cinnamon, cloves, allspice, coriander and cardamon, care with the ginger, and the brake definitely on the peppers and mustard.

APPLES

4 lbs. of sour apples.	3 inches of cinnamon stick.
1½ pints of spirit or cider vinegar.	1 teaspoonful of allspice.
2 lbs. of sugar.	20 whole cloves.

Peel and core the apples, putting them in water till wanted to stop discoloration.

Boil the vinegar, sugar and spices together for five minutes, then add the apples and simmer till just tender but not soft. Take out the fruit and pack it into the jars, then reboil the vinegar and sugar till a syrup is formed. Pour into the jars and close whilst hot. The spices may be added to the jars or strained out, whichever you prefer.

If the apples are too large they should be halved or quartered.

SPICED CRAB APPLES

As crabs can be gathered from almost any hedgerow and are excellent spiced, some should always be pickled during the late summer. Spiced malt vinegar may be used if the spicing is not too hot.

> 5 lbs. of crab apples of even size.
> 2½ lbs. of sugar.
> 1 quart of spiced vinegar.

Wipe the crabs in a damp cloth and remove any stalks but do not peel. Add the sugar to the vinegar and bring to the boil, then put in the apples and simmer till tender. Take care not to overdo this, for once they start to break up it will be a jelly and not a pickle we shall end with. Take them from the vinegar and pack into jars. Reboil the liquor until a syrup is formed, then fill the jars full. A few pieces of ginger root may be added if you like that flavour.

APRICOTS

Definitely a luxury pickle, apricots are best prepared in their jars—and glass-topped ones at that.

5 lbs. of apricots.	1 teaspoonful of whole allspice.
1 quart of distilled vinegar.	3 pieces of white ginger.
3 lbs. of white sugar.	12 whole cloves.
3 inches of cinnamon stick.	

Cut the apricots in half and remove the stones, then pack them, not too tightly, into glass jars and place in the oven with the glass top on the jars but without the rubber band. Leave them till the skin is just beginning to peel, but take them out before they start to pulp.

In the meantime boil the vinegar, sugar and spices together until a thick syrup is formed, then pour this onto the fruit as you take it from the oven.

Allow the jars to stand for a few minutes, shaking a little to remove air bubbles, then fill up with syrup, replace the rubber band and close securely whilst still hot.

BARBERRIES

Barberries are the orange-red berries of the Berberis, and Mrs. Glasse gives instructions for pickling them. That they can be done safely is confirmed by the *Encyclopædia Britannica*, which says : " The berries of the Berberis are edible : those of the native Barberry are sometimes made into preserve."

Personally I have never pickled them, but here is the recipe for anyone who cares to try—though as usual Hannah Glasse is very vague about her quantities, so the formula has been simplified.

To one quart of distilled vinegar add half a pound of sugar and a quarter of a pound of salt.

Divide the barberries into two portions, placing the largest and soundest fruit into jars. The others add to the vinegar and boil until the liquor is a good colour, skimming off the scum as it rises.

Decant the vinegar off and allow it to cool and settle, then pour the clear liquid onto the barberries in jars, throwing the boiled ones away.

She also suggests a sprig of fennel in the top of each jar.

BLACKBERRIES

Considering that they can be got for the picking, it is surprising blackberries are not more frequently spiced.

> 5 lbs. of firm blackberries.
> 2 lbs. of sugar.
> 1 pint of aromatic spiced vinegar.

Malt vinegar may be used for these, or you may use unspiced vinegar, but then add :

> $\frac{1}{2}$ oz. of whole cloves.
> $\frac{1}{2}$ oz. of cinnamon stick.
> $\frac{1}{2}$ oz. of allspice berries.

Boil the sugar, vinegar and spices together for five minutes, then remove the spices and add the blackberries. Simmer for five minutes, take out the fruit and put it into warmed jars. Then boil up the liquor till a syrup is formed, and pour over the berries. Close securely whilst still hot. A little ginger root may be added to the spices if desired.

CHERRIES

Another neglected pickle which is well worth making, for, like Swiss Cherry Jam, once tasted it is never forgotten.

4 lbs. of cherries.	3 inches of cinnamon stick.
2 lbs. of white sugar.	4 pieces of white ginger.
1 pint of spirit vinegar.	6 cloves.

Either stone or split the cherries. Boil the vinegar, sugar and spices together for five minutes, then remove the spices. Put in the cherries, simmer for five minutes, then transfer the fruit to warmed jars. Boil up the liquor till a syrup forms, then pour over the fruit. Close whilst still hot.

Alternatively the cherries may be placed in their jars and heated in the oven and the hot syrup poured over in the same way as for apricots.

An American method is to cover the cherries with cold syrup, allow them to stand a week, then reboil the syrup and cover the cherries with it when cold; but it is doubtful if this double boiling shows any advantage.

SPICED DATES

Dates are used extensively in commercial sauce manufacture. They are cheap and make a fair sweet pickle, though it is not everyone who likes the flavour. Owing to their naturally high sugar content, none need be added.

4 lbs. of dried dates.
¼ lb. of salt.
1 quart of mixed spiced vinegar.

Stone the dates and pack them loosely in jars, then place these in the oven and warm through but don't cook. Add the salt to the vinegar and bring to the boil, fill up the jars and close down whilst hot.

They must be watched during storage for signs of fermentation, as this sticky fruit picks up spores readily.

DAMSONS

All the plums pickle well and damsons are no exception, but care must be taken that they are not overcooked.

Like all the soft fruits they are easiest to do in the jars, as transferring from one vessel to another tends to break them up. Mixed spice malt vinegar is satisfactory, as a deep colour does not matter. They are, however, rather greedy of sugar.

> 4 lbs. of damsons.
> 2 lbs. of sugar (preferably brown).
> 1 pint of spiced vinegar.

Place the fruit in their jars and heat in the oven till the skins split. Boil the vinegar and sugar into a syrup, take the jars from the oven and pour the hot syrup over the fruit. Close immediately and mature for two weeks before using ; they will be even better in two months.

SPICED FIGS

Figs are rather difficult to pickle, as they are so likely to burst and then the hundreds of seeds make rather a messy-looking jar.

Pick the fruit before it is fully ripe, pack into jars and warm through in the oven.

Make a syrup of one pound of sugar and one quart of spiced malt vinegar, boiling until it thickens, then pour it on the warmed figs and close whilst hot.

Some recipes advise decanting the liquor off after a week's storage, reboiling and pouring over the fruit again.

Owing to their shape, figs take rather a lot of syrup, and it is really much simpler to enjoy them as fresh fruit.

PICKLED GOOSEBERRIES

The gooseberry comes into its own as a chutney, and a number of recipes for these will be found in that section. When pickled whole they are liable to shrivel unless well cooked, and the difficulty then is to stop them breaking up into chutney anyway. The best method is to do them as a stewed fruit.

> 5 lbs. of gooseberries.
> 3 lbs. of sugar.
> 1 quart of spiced spirit or malt vinegar.

Top and tail the gooseberries and place them with the sugar and vinegar in the preserving pan.

Heat until simmering and simmer till the fruit is tender. Don't boil or the gooseberries will burst. Take the fruit out carefully and pack into warmed jars, then reheat the liquor until it forms a syrup and fill the jars full.

Close whilst still hot.

It is, of course, only green gooseberries that can be pickled.

GRAPES

It is a waste to pickle hot-house grapes, they are too great a delicacy, but in most villages vines of the old-fashioned " Sweetwater " can be found rambling up the walls of some old cottage. They are excellent spiced.

Pick the grapes carefully, discarding any that are bruised or that have been attacked by wasps, pack them into jars and warm the jars in the oven.

Prepare a pickle of one pound of sugar to one quart of vinegar, preferably using spirit vinegar and aromatic spicing, and boil this to a thin syrup. Pour into the jars and seal whilst hot.

Alternatively the grapes can be simmered in the syrup until tender in the same way as for gooseberries, but they are rather more difficult to transfer to their jars without breaking.

LEMONS

Lemons are too dear to pickle in any quantity, but *Domestic Cookery* gives an interesting recipe.

No sugar is used and the pickle is very sharp in taste, but is one of the few that goes well with fish.

Select small lemons with thick rinds. Slit them lengthwise in quarters, but don't cut right through. Rub dry salt into these cuts and brine the lemons for five days, or until all the salt has melted, turning them in the liquor which forms. Drain off this liquor and add to it enough vinegar to cover the lemons completely, then boil it up with whole pepper and a little ginger. Skim off the scum whilst boiling, allow the pickle to cool and pour it over the fruit, adding to each jar two ounces of mustard seed and two cloves of garlic to every six lemons.

The good lady adds : " When the lemons are used the pickle will be useful in fish and other sauces."

Owing to the amount of pepper and mustard this pickle is very hot and a little goes a long way.

6

SPICED NECTARINES

If nectarines are to be pickled at all they are worthy of a little extra trouble.

25 nectarines.	1 oz. of whole cloves.
2 lbs. of best white sugar.	1 oz. of cardamon seed.
1½ pints of distilled malt vinegar.	1 oz. of cinnamon.

Select fruit that is not too ripe. Dip each nectarine into hot water for a few moments and peel carefully. Cut each in half and remove the stone and place these in the oven to dry.

Add the sugar to the vinegar and tie the spices in a muslin bag, and place all in the preserving pan and bring to the boil. Boil until a thin syrup forms and to this add the nectarines.

Simmer till just tender, but in the meantime crack the stones and remove the kernels, adding these to the pickle for the last few minutes.

When tender but not soft, remove the fruit carefully and pack it, the cut sides uppermost, into warmed jars, putting in the kernels.

Now remove the bag of spices and boil up the syrup once more till it is thick. Pour over the fruit and close securely whilst hot.

They should be delicious, but so they are fresh !

Crack the stones and remove kernels.

PICKLED PEACHES

The best pickled peach is made from fresh fruit, but this is always expensive and not always available. Quite a satisfactory substitute can be made from either tinned or dried peaches, and recipes for all three kinds are given.

I. Fresh Peaches

6 lbs. of peaches.	1 oz. of cloves.
3 lbs. of white sugar.	1 oz. of allspice.
1½ pints of distilled malt vinegar.	1 oz. of cinnamon stick.

Dip the peaches into hot water and peel them, then cut in half and remove the stones, crack these and take out the kernels.

Tie the spices in a muslin bag and boil the vinegar, sugar and spices together. When the liquor is boiling, put in the halved peaches and simmer till tender. Remove them carefully and place into warmed jars, boil up the pickle again to a thick syrup and pour over the fruit. Close whilst hot and store for at least a week before using.

2. Tinned Peaches

Separate the peaches from the syrup and pack them into jars. Measure the quantity of syrup and then make a fresh syrup in the proportions of one pint of spiced vinegar and one pound of sugar, boiling down to the same consistency as the original.

Pour onto the peaches whilst hot and seal well.

Another way is to add to the original syrup an equal quantity of spiced vinegar and sugar, again boiling to the original thickness, but as this makes nearly double the quantity required it is wasteful, unless other fruits are being pickled at the same time.

In either case the peaches are ready to eat in a few days and should not be kept too long.

3. Dried Peaches

Dried fruits are simple to pickle, as the water has already been extracted, and can be very successful. They need soaking in the vinegar for forty-eight hours before the pickle is actually made—indeed, the process is similar to stewing, except that vinegar is used in place of water.

> 2 lbs. of dried peaches.
> 4 lbs. of sugar.
> 3 quarts of spiced vinegar.

General mixed spiced malt vinegar is best and the peaches must be laid in pie-dishes and covered with vinegar for forty-eight hours. They will absorb a good deal of vinegar and at the end of the first day it may be necessary to add more.

When they are nicely swollen, pour off the vinegar and to it add the sugar, then bring to the boil in the preserving pan, then add the peaches and simmer till tender. Take them out carefully and place in warmed jars, boil up the liquor to a medium thick syrup and pour, hot, onto the peaches. Seal immediately and allow them to mature for a week before use. If the closure is airtight they will keep for months.

PLUMS

Plums require a fair amount of sugar and should be pickled in their jars. Choose firm, unbruised fruit and pack them carefully ; the actual quantities will vary rather with the type and size of the plums, but an average recipe would be :

> 4 lbs. of plums.
> 2 lbs. of sugar.
> 2 pints of spiced vinegar.

Place the jars with the plums in them in a medium oven and heat through. Then make a syrup of the sugar and spiced vinegar, and pour, boiling, into the hot jars. Seal immediately and mature for three weeks before opening.

PEARS

Pears are rather tricky things to pickle as they so easily break when overcooked, but don't let this fact stop you trying some, for they can be delicious.

Only hard, cooking pears should be used; the small kinds may be pickled whole but the larger varieties should be halved or quartered and the cores removed.

> 5 lbs. of prepared pears.
> 2 lbs. of sugar.
> 1 quart of pale spiced vinegar.

Peel the pears and into each stick one whole clove. Boil the sugar and vinegar together and put in the pears, a few at a time, cooking each lot for a few minutes only. Take them out as soon as they start to look transparent and place them in warmed jars. Boil up the liquor again to a thin syrup and pour into the warmed jars. Seal immediately. This is a West Country recipe and a note to it adds : " In a couple of weeks they are ready for serving with pork in place of apple sauce."

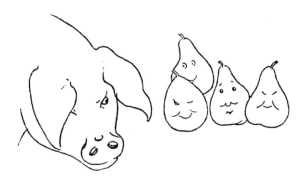

PRUNES

In many countries prunes are eaten with meat, and they can be pickled in the same manner as dried peaches. They must be soaked in spiced vinegar for forty-eight hours first, but need much less sugar in the final pickle.

2 lbs. of prunes.
½ lb. of sugar.
1 quart of spiced vinegar.

Soak the prunes in the vinegar, then strain, and add the sugar to the vinegar. Bring to the boil in the preserving pan, put in the prunes and simmer till tender. Pack into jars and cover with the hot syrup which will be thick enough without any extra boiling.

They may also be stewed in the oven in the vinegar and sugar, but the dishes must be covered and the cooking done slowly.

One quince in apple pie makes an entirely different thing of it.

QUINCE

Many people have never even seen a quince, but they were used quite a lot years ago; their characteristic flavour gives variety to many other fruits. One quince in an apple pie makes an entirely different thing of it. They pickle well but, like pears, easily break up if overcooked.

> 2 lbs. of prepared quince.
> 1 lb. of sugar.
> 1 pint of spiced vinegar.

Peel and core the quince and divide into quarters. Boil up the vinegar and sugar to a thin syrup, then add the quince and simmer gently till tender.

Pack into warmed jars and cover with the syrup. Close whilst still hot and keep for a fortnight before opening.

RHUBARB

Considering the amount of rhubarb grown in kitchen gardens and allotments, it is surprising one does not find it spiced more often.

The process is simple, and in this case the fruit needs to be well cooked.

> 3 lbs. of rhubarb.
> 2 lbs. of sugar.
> 1 pint of spiced vinegar.
> a little extra clove, cinnamon and ginger.

The extra spices are necessary, as during the longer cooking some of their flavour will evaporate.

Cut the rhubarb into inch pieces and simmer with the sugar, spices and vinegar till the rhubarb is transparent. Then remove the fruit and reboil the liquor until it is a thick syrup. The final pickle, when cold, should be almost a jelly. Close while still hot and it is ready to eat in a couple of days.

CHUTNEYS AND
KETCHUPS

*The boiling together of fruit, spices and vinegar is apt to make the house smell
like a factory.*

CHUTNEYS AND KETCHUPS

CHUTNEYS and the chutney type of mixed pickle have become very popular in recent years. They are easy to make at home and should appeal to the housewife, as a few hours will see the whole process through.

Many cannot be bought at all as, owing to the uncertainty in the supply of the fruit, commercial picklers hesitate to market them.

There is only one snag : the boiling together of fruit, spices and vinegar is apt to make the whole house smell like a factory. Therefore prepare them when the family is out, keep the kitchen door shut and the window open. Then produce your chutney as a surprise ! It will be welcomed.

In practically all chutneys unspiced vinegar is used, and the spices, either whole or ground, are mixed in with the other ingredients. Chutneys should be filled into their jars whilst hot, and therefore the jars must be thoroughly warmed or they will crack. All chutneys improve with keeping and some may be kept for two or three years with safety.

There is one useful tip for making chutneys. In commercial practice, trial lots are periodically run through to test the quality and flavour of the different materials. Wherever possible the housewife should follow this system at home. As an example, if you are proposing to make ten pounds or more of green-goose-berry chutney, do one pound first and see how you like it. This will enable you to vary the spicing to suit your own taste, so that when you prepare the main supply you can add more sugar or use less salt, increase the ginger or take out the cloves, for no two people's taste is quite the same, and a recipe is only how somebody else liked it and may not appeal to your particular family.

APPLE CHUTNEYS

I. Apple Chutney

6 lbs. of apples.	1 teaspoonful of allspice.
3½ lbs. of sugar.	1 oz. of salt.
2 lbs. of sultanas.	3 pints of vinegar.
¾ lbs. of preserved ginger.	

Peel, core and chop the apples into small pieces and chop up the sultanas and ginger. Mix the vinegar, sugar, salt and spices together and bring to the boil, then add the apples and simmer for ten minutes before adding the ginger and sultanas. Simmer until the mixture becomes fairly thick, then pour into the jars.

2. Apple Chutney

3 lbs. of apples.	2 ozs. of salt.
1 lb. of onions.	½ oz. of curry powder.
1 lb. of stoned raisins.	2 tablespoonsful of treacle.
1 lb. of currants.	½ a teaspoonful of ground ginger.
2 lbs. of brown sugar.	1 pint of vinegar.
2 ozs. of mustard.	

Peel and core the apples and chop finely, then chop the onions and raisins. Place all the ingredients, except the ginger, mustard and curry powder, in the preserving pan and simmer gently until a brown colour. Add the ginger, mustard and curry powder when nearly done. Bottle hot and tie down closely.

3. Apple Chutney

1 lb. of sour apples.	¾ oz. of cayenne pepper.
½ lb. of raisins.	7 ozs. of brown sugar.
6 ozs. of shallots or onions.	3 ozs. of salt.
1 oz. of ground ginger.	1 pint of vinegar.

Peel and core the apples, then chop very finely with the raisins. Add all the other ingredients and mix well and allow to stand one hour. Then simmer for half an hour or until the chutney thickens. Bottle whilst hot.

It is impossible to give all the recipes for chutney in which apples take a prominent part; many people have their own method, often handed down from other generations and rather a "secret," and some of these will be found under "Indian Chutneys," whilst the following recipes give some indication of the sort of mixtures that can be made.

APPLE AND TOMATO CHUTNEY

3 lbs. of apples.
3 lbs. of tomatoes.
1 lb. of onions.
1 lb. of sugar.

½ oz. of white peppercorns.
1 oz. of ground ginger.
1 quart of vinegar.
2 ozs. of salt.

Peel, core and slice the apples. Peel the onions and chop finely and slice the tomatoes thinly. Place these in a large bowl and cover with the vinegar. Allow them to stand for twenty-four hours, then transfer to the preserving pan and add the sugar, spices and salt.

Bring all to the boil and simmer for half an hour or until tender. Bottle whilst hot and close securely.

APPLE AND MARROW CHUTNEY

3 lbs. of prepared marrow.
1 lb. of onions.
1½ lbs. of apples.
1 lb. of sugar.

1 oz. of peppercorns.
½ oz. of allspice.
1 quart of vinegar.

One of the few chutneys in which brining is necessary. Peel and cut the marrow into small squares, sprinkle with dry salt and stand for twenty-four hours, then drain well.

Peel and core the apples and slice into thin pieces, chop the onions finely and cook these three together in half the vinegar until tender, then add the rest of the vinegar and spices and simmer until the whole mass thickens. Bottle whilst hot and seal well.

APPLE AND PLUM CHUTNEY

1 lb. of apples.	1 lb. of sugar.
3 lbs. of plums.	¼ lb. of salt.
1 lb. of chopped carrot or turnip.	1 teaspoonful of cloves.
	1 teaspoonful of cinnamon.
1 lb. of raisins.	1 teaspoonful of ground ginger.
½ lb. of onions.	1 teaspoonful of allspice.

Peel, core and chop the apples finely. Take the stones from the plums and cut the fruit into quarters, then chop the onions and raisins finely.

Boil the vinegar, sugar and spices together and, when boiling, add the apples, plums and carrot or turnip. Boil until the mixture thickens, and bottle whilst hot.

This is rather an aromatic chutney and is quite a good substitute for red-currant jelly. The spices may be varied to suit individual taste.

APPLE AND DATE CHUTNEY

1 lb. of apples.	2 tablespoonsful of sugar.
2 lbs. of dates.	4 ozs. of salt.
½ lb. of sultanas.	1 saltspoonful of cayenne pepper.
1 lb. of onions.	2½ pints of vinegar.
1 lb. of treacle.	

Peel and core the apples and stone the dates. Peel the onions and then put all the fruit and onions through the mincer.

Add the treacle, sugar, salt and spices to the vinegar ; bring to the boil, then add the minced fruit and simmer for three-quarters of an hour or until thick, and bottle hot.

APPLE AND BANANA

2 lbs. of apples.	1 level teaspoonful of ground ginger.
1 doz. bananas.	1 level teaspoonful of cinnamon.
¾ lb. of onions.	1 oz. of curry powder.
½ lb. of raisins.	½ oz. of cayenne pepper.
2 ozs. of salt.	1 pint of vinegar.

Peel, core and chop the apples and onions finely. Skin the bananas and cut into sections and cut the raisins in half.

Mix the sugar, salt and spices with the vinegar, bring to the boil and then add the fruit. Simmer gently for two hours (stirring well as the bananas burn easily), or until the apples are tender and the chutney thick. Bottle hot and seal closely.

BANANA CHUTNEY

1 doz. bananas.	2 ozs. of salt.
½ lb. of stoned raisins.	½ oz. of powdered cinnamon.
¼ lb. of currants.	1 oz. of curry powder.
½ lb. of sugar.	1 pint of vinegar.

If preferred, one pound of sultanas may be substituted for the raisins and currants.

Peel and slice the bananas, add them to the vinegar and boil until the consistency of porridge. Then add the fruit and spices and simmer for a further quarter of an hour (the raisins may be chopped or not).

This is a very mild chutney, and if the curry powder is left out it is suitable for the young, only then it really is rather insipid.

BEETROOT CHUTNEY

3 lbs. of prepared beetroot.	½ oz. of salt.
1 lb. of stoned raisins.	1 oz. of allspice.
½ lb. of onions.	½ teaspoonful of pepper.
½ lb. of sugar.	1 pint of vinegar.

This chutney takes rather longer to make as the beetroot must first be cooked in a standard brine until tender Then skin carefully and chop into very small pieces. Chop the onions and raisins finely and add them to the vinegar with the sugar and spices. Boil until the onion is tender and the mixture starting to thicken, then put in the chopped beetroot and simmer for a further quarter of an hour.

This is rather a sweet chutney but is an interesting variant to the sliced beetroot.

BEETROOT AND RED CABBAGE CHUTNEY

These two vegetables make a good dark-red chutney which goes excellently with all cold meats. It should not be made for long storage as, unlike nearly all the other chutneys, it is apt to deteriorate, the colour sometimes turning to dark brown.

2 lbs. of shredded red cabbage.	1 lb. of sugar.
2 lbs. of uncooked beetroot.	2 ozs. of peppercorns.
½ lb. of onions.	2 ozs. of mustard seed.
¼ lb. of salt.	1 quart of vinegar.

Shred the cabbage and chop finely. Peel and chop the raw beetroot into small squares and chop the onion as fine as possible or put it through the mincer.

Add all the other ingredients to the vinegar and boil, then put in the chopped vegetables and simmer gently until thoroughly tender. Bottle whilst hot and seal well. If it is liked sharper in flavour, the sugar may be omitted.

CRANBERRY CHUTNEY

An unfamiliar chutney to the English housewife, though in America, where cranberry sauce is essential for the Thanksgiving turkey, it is quite popular.

3 lbs. of cranberries.	3 pieces of ginger.
1 lb. of raisins.	½ oz. of allspice.
½ lb. of sultanas.	1 oz. of salt.
½ lb. of sugar.	1 pint of vinegar.
½ oz. of powdered cinnamon.	

Put the cranberries in the preserving pan and just cover with vinegar, then simmer until tender. Add the other ingredients and continue to cook until a thick mixture is formed. Bottle hot and close securely.

7

DATE CHUTNEY

3 lbs. of dates.	2 ozs. of salt.
1 lb. of spring onions.	1 oz. of allspice.
½ lb. of raisins.	½ oz. of mustard seed.
¼ lb. of currants.	1 quart of vinegar.
½ lb. of sugar.	

Stone and cut the dates into small pieces and cut the onions finely as far as the green tops, but don't put these in. Chop the raisins, then put all the materials into a preserving pan and cook thoroughly till a thick mixture forms. Bottle hot and seal closely.

If spring onions are not in season, mild Spanish onions may be used instead.

ELDERBERRY CHUTNEY

3 lbs. of elderberries.	1 teaspoonful of powdered cinnamon.
½ lb. of sultanas.	
½ lb. of onions.	1 teaspoonful of allspice.
½ lb. of sugar.	1 teaspoonful of cayenne pepper.
1 teaspoonful of ground ginger.	¼ lb. of salt.
	1 pint of vinegar.

Pick the berries before they are ripe, take them off the stalks, add them to the vinegar and start to heat. In the meantime chop the onion finely and when the berries are starting to boil, add all the other ingredients. Continue to simmer until the berries break and the mixture thickens. Bottle hot and close well.

GOOSEBERRY CHUTNEYS

One of the most popular home-made chutneys, for which there are many recipes. Three examples are given but there is no need to be governed by them. Gooseberries blend well in almost any proportions, owing to their natural sharpness, so if you have a well-tried recipe of your own, stick to it.

1. Gooseberry Chutney

2 lbs. of green gooseberries.
1 lb. of stoned raisins.
¾ lb. of onions.
1 lb. of sugar.

3 ozs. of pounded mustard seed.
1 oz. of salt.
1 teaspoonful of cayenne pepper.

Chop the onions finely and cut the raisins in half. Boil the gooseberries, onions and sugar together for three-quarters of an hour, then add the raisins, salt and pepper. Simmer for five minutes, then bottle.

2. Gooseberry Chutney

4 lbs. of gooseberries.
1½ lbs. of stoned raisins.
1 lb. of onions.
1 lb. of moist sugar.

¼ lb. of mustard seed.
2 ozs. of allspice.
1 quart of vinegar.
¼ lb. of salt.

Bruise the mustard seed gently. Mix the sugar with one pint of vinegar and boil until a syrup forms, then add the finely chopped onions, raisins and spices.

Boil the gooseberries in the rest of the vinegar until tender, then mix both lots together and cook until it thickens. Bottle and tie down tightly.

A note to this says : " The longer kept the better."

3. Gooseberry Chutney

4 lbs. of green gooseberries.
1 lb. of stoned raisins or sultanas.
2 lbs. of sugar.
1 tablespoonful of treacle.
1 lb. of onions.
2 ozs. of mustard seed.

2 ozs. of ground ginger.
4 ozs. of salt.
1 teaspoonful of cayenne.
1 teaspoonful of turmeric.
3 pints of vinegar.

Chop the onions and raisins finely and cut the gooseberries in half. Crush the mustard seed, then mix everything together except the turmeric and simmer for one hour, then add the turmeric and continue to cook until tender.

This also improves with keeping and should therefore be bottled hot.

INDIAN CHUTNEYS

This was the ancestor of all our chutneys (the word itself comes from the Hindustani, *chatni*) and in their original form Indian chutneys are made from mangoes, tamarinds and other tropical fruits and spices, many of which are difficult or impossible to obtain in this country. Apples, raisins and sultanas can make quite passable substitutes, though in the following four recipes one is for the proper mango chutney.

I. Mango Chutney

4 lbs. of peeled and quartered mangoes.
3 lbs. of peeled and chopped apples.
½ lb. of stoned dates.
¼ lb. of sultanas.
¼ lb. of finely chopped onion.
2 ozs. of salt.
2 lemons (the juice only),

½ oz. of cayenne pepper
½ teaspoonful of nutmeg.
6 bay leaves.
1 quart of vinegar (bottled 5 per cent.).
4 lbs. of sugar.
1 fluid oz. of lime juice.

Fourteen ingredients and the weights are for prepared materials. Place them all, except the sugar and lime juice, in a large bowl and mix thoroughly, then let them stand for three hours. Transfer to the preserving pan and bring to the boil, then simmer until tender, stirring all the time. Finally add the sugar and lime juice and continue to simmer until the whole mass thickens. Bottle hot and close securely.

The longer it is matured the better.

2. Indian Chutney

8 lbs. of apples.
4 lbs. of sultanas.
2 lbs. of stoned raisins.
8 lbs. of brown sugar.
1 lb. of salt.

4 ozs. of garlic.
4 ozs. of red chillies.
8 ozs. of mustard seed.
2 quarts of vinegar.

This is a recipe from the old East India Company, in which apples replace mangoes.

Peel and slice the apples, mix with the salt and allow to stand twenty-four hours. The next day put the sultanas, raisins, garlic and chillies through a fine mincer and pound the mustard and ginger together.

To the other quart of vinegar add the sugar and simmer till a syrup is formed, then add the mustard and ginger and simmer for five minutes; then add the minced dried fruits, garlic and chillies, and finally the apples and vinegar. Mix thoroughly and simmer until thick, then fill into warmed jars and tie down. If an aromatic flavour is liked, an ounce of ground cloves and an ounce of allspice may be added.

Here again long maturing is an advantage, for it will keep almost indefinitely—I know of some five years old; but it is a very hot mixture, a little goes a long way, and it is meant for colonels and not children!

It is meant for colonels and not children.

3. Indian Chutney

2 lbs. of apples.	½ oz. of ground ginger.
1 lb. of green tomatoes.	½ oz. of allspice.
1 lb. of stoned raisins.	½ oz. of turmeric.
½ lb. of sultanas.	2 lbs. of sugar.
½ lb. of onions.	¼ lb. of salt.
6 ozs. of almonds.	1 quart of vinegar.
1 teaspoonful of mustard.	

A rather milder flavoured chutney. The apples must be peeled and cored, then put all the solid ingredients through a fine mincer. Add them to the vinegar, sugar and spices, and let them stand twenty-four hours.

Then transfer to a preserving pan and simmer gently for from two to three hours, until the mixture is thick. Fill into warmed jars and close securely.

4. Indian Chutney

5 lbs. of apples.	1 teaspoonful of ground ginger.
1 lb. of onions.	1 teaspoonful of dry mustard.
1 lb. of raisins.	1 teaspoonful of bruised allspice.
1 lb. of sultanas.	1 quart of vinegar.
1 lb. of sugar.	2 ozs. of salt.

The simplest recipe, but requires long and gentle cooking. Peel, core and slice the apples, then put the apples, onions, raisins and sultanas through a mincer.

Add all the other ingredients to the vinegar and bring to the boil, then put in the minced fruit and simmer gently until the mass thickens. Bottle whilst hot and close well. Like all Indian chutneys, maturing is beneficial.

Drain the apples from the brine and boil in one quart of the vinegar till tender, then allow to cool.

LEMON CHUTNEY

Lemon chutney is rather an acquired taste, but it is popular in some of the Colonies and goes well with curry as a variant to the Indian chutney.

1 lb. of lemons.	4 ozs. of sultanas.
4 medium onions.	1 oz. of chillies.
1 lb. of sugar.	2 ozs. of salt.
4 ozs. of raisins.	1½ pints of vinegar.

Squeeze the lemons and save the juice, then cut the rind small and put through a fine mincer, taking out the pips or not as you prefer. Chop the onions and raisins finely and the chillies as small as possible, then mix all the ingredients together and let them stand for a few hours. Next transfer to a preserving pan and simmer gently till thick.

Bottle whilst hot and close well. This should be kept at least a month before opening.

Incidentally this recipe can be adapted to other citrus fruits such as Seville oranges, grape-fruit, limes, etc. ; but it is essential to make a trial batch, as these fruits vary greatly in flavour and the amount of juice present, so no standard recipe is of much use.

MARROW CHUTNEY

The vegetable marrow is a useful foundation for chutneys; it has already been given mixed with apples, but it should be brined first.

5 lbs. of marrow.	¼ lb. of sugar.
½ lb. of onions.	½ oz. of ground ginger.
½ lb. of raisins.	1 oz. of mustard seed.
½ lb. of sultanas.	1 quart of vinegar.
½ lb. of currants.	

Peel the marrow and cut it into small pieces, lay them in a deep bowl and sprinkle each layer with salt, then let it stand for twenty-four hours.

Chop the onion, add it to the dried fruits, then put all these through a fine mincer. Next, pound the mustard seed and add this with the sugar and ginger to the vinegar, and bring to the boil. Then put in the marrow, after well draining, and finally the minced fruits and onion. Simmer gently for one and a half to two hours or until the mixture is thick. Other spices may be added to this if their flavour is liked—cinnamon and allspice go well.

Bottle whilst hot, and tie down.

PEACH CHUTNEY

Dried peaches, or for that matter dried apricots, may be utilized as the base for chutney, and owing to their low water but high sugar content they keep well.

2 lbs. of dried peaches.	½ oz. of powdered cinnamon.
1 lb. of onions.	½ oz. of ground ginger.
1 lb. of raisins.	1 quart of vinegar.
½ lb. of sultanas.	

Cut the peaches into quarters, lay them in a shallow pan and cover with cold vinegar. Let them stand twenty-four hours, or until the fruit has swollen.

Chop the onions finely and cut the raisins in half, then add them with the spices to the rest of the vinegar; bring to the boil and simmer for fifteen minutes.

Then put in the peaches and vinegar, and continue to cook until thick.

Bottle hot, and close securely. It will be better for at least a fortnight's storage before use.

PLUM CHUTNEY

Plums are usually mixed with apples and onions in chutney, and a recipe for this type has been given; yet they can make a very good mild chutney on their own, and the process amounts to little more than stewing the plums in spiced vinegar.

5 lbs. of plums.	1 oz. of powdered cinnamon.
2 lbs. of sugar.	1 oz. of allspice.
3 ozs. of salt.	1 oz. of bruised mustard seed.
1 oz. of ground ginger.	1 quart of vinegar.

Stone the plums and cut into quarters. Add all the other ingredients to the vinegar and bring to the boil, then put in the plums and simmer till tender. If the mixture is still too thin, continue to simmer gently until the desired consistency is obtained.

Can Rhubarb truly be called a fruit?

RHUBARB CHUTNEY

A great deal of rhubarb is wasted, as it is the first fruit (if it can truly be called a fruit) that appears. So by the time gooseberries, currants and the full summer's harvest comes in, people are tired of rhubarb and cease to pull it. It is then that some should be put into chutney; it mixes quite well with gooseberries and plums, and its natural acidity makes it a good keeping chutney.

4 lbs. of rhubarb.	1 oz. of salt.
1 lb. of raisins.	½ oz. of allspice.
1 lb. of apples.	½ oz. of ginger.
1 lb. of onions.	½ oz. of bruised mustard seed.
1 lb. of sugar.	1½ pints of vinegar.

Clean the rhubarb and cut it into small pieces. Put the onions and raisins through a mincer and chop the apples finely. Then mix the sugar, salt and spices with the vinegar, bring to the boil, add the fruit and onions, and simmer gently till well cooked and thick. This will take about two hours. Bottle hot, and close securely.

TOMATO CHUTNEYS

Tomatoes, whether green or red, make the simplest and probably most popular of the home-made chutneys.

Many recipes are needlessly involved, and the easiest way is the best, and produces quite as good a chutney.

This consists in slicing the tomatoes thinly, mixing with all the other materials and simmering until the mixture is the right thickness. To add a little variety, however, some of the other methods are given.

1. Green Tomato Chutney

2 lbs. of green tomatoes.	4 teaspoonsful of mustard seed.
1 lb. of sliced onions.	$\frac{1}{2}$ teaspoonful of ground ginger.
4 tablespoonsful of sugar.	$\frac{1}{2}$ teaspoonful of cayenne pepper.
2 tablespoonsful of salt.	1 pint of vinegar.

Slice the tomatoes and onions and mix them in a stone jar, then mix all the other ingredients in the vinegar and pour, cold, into the jar. Place the jar in a slow oven for three hours. Then tie down well.

2. Green Tomato Chutney

5 lbs. of green tomatoes.	1 lb. of sugar.
1 lb. of onions.	$\frac{1}{2}$ oz. of peppercorns.
$\frac{1}{2}$ lb. of sultanas.	1 oz. of salt.
$\frac{1}{2}$ lb. of raisins.	1 quart of vinegar.

Slice the tomatoes and chop the onion and mix together in a basin with the pepper and salt. Allow this to stand over-night. Next day boil up the sugar in the vinegar, then add the raisins (which may be chopped) and the sultanas. Simmer for five minutes, then add the tomatoes and onions, and simmer till thick.

3. Red Tomato Chutney

2 lbs. of ripe tomatoes.	½ oz. of salt.
1 lb. of apples.	¼ oz. of ground ginger.
½ lb. of raisins.	¼ teaspoonful of ground cloves.
1 lb. of brown sugar.	¼ teaspoonful of cayenne pepper.
1 large onion.	1 pint of vinegar.

Dip the tomatoes in boiling water and skin carefully, then cut them up finely. Chop the onion, apples and raisins as small as possible, or put through a mincer.

Then mix everything together in the vinegar, place in the preserving pan and boil for one hour.

Bottle whilst hot, and close well.

4. Red Tomato Chutney

3 lbs. of ripe tomatoes.	¼ oz. of pepper.
1 lb. of sugar.	¼ oz. of mustard seed.
½ lb. of shallots.	½ teaspoonful of allspice.
½ lb. of sultanas.	1½ pints of vinegar.
1 oz. of salt.	

Dip the tomatoes in boiling water and skin, then chop finely, chop the shallots, mixing both together.

Add all the other ingredients to the vinegar and bring to the boil, then add the tomatoes and shallots and simmer slowly until it becomes really thick.

Bottle hot, and keep for two weeks before using.

That list does not by any means exhaust the chutney recipes, which vary greatly. But all have this in common, that the ingredients are thoroughly cooked until the right thickness is obtained—everything else is merely variation to get the flavour you like.

Many other fruits will make chutney—for instance, quince or tamarind or many of the tropical fruits that are seldom seen here, guava pears and passion fruit, but . . . one cannot grow these on an allotment !

KETCHUPS

The great British Public has never made up its mind how to spell this word, for as often as not it is given as Catsup, Catchup or even Katchup. Like Chutney, it is of Eastern origin and is derived from the Chinese " Koe-chiap " or " Ke-tsiap," the brine of pickled fish.

It was first used in this country to describe a sauce made from mushrooms (it was probably introduced by the East India Company in this form), but later walnuts and other fruits and vegetables were used as a base, whilst to-day if one merely asked for " Ketchup " it is a hundred to one that some form of tomato sauce would be brought.

Ketchups are not too easy to make and even harder to keep. The safest method is to sterilize in the bottles by heating to 170° F. and holding at that temperature for at least fifteen minutes, then closing securely whilst still hot.

The trouble is that the quantities of vinegar, sugar and salt used in their preparation does not produce a high enough concentration to stop fermentation, whilst any varying of the quantity that would achieve this spoils the flavour of the ketchup.

It is important to see that the bottles used are perfectly clean and that the corks or stoppers are new and have themselves been sterilized in hot water.

It will be quite useless sterilizing bottles of tomato ketchup for two hours, then closing them with old, infected corks. They will blow up in a week or two like ginger beer that has been bottled too soon.

Ketchups require straining at some stage in their preparation, and this should not be done through a wire sieve, which will be iron. A hair sieve or a piece of coarse butter-muslin stretched across a basin should be used.

The spicing is more important with ketchups than with any other form of pickling, so a small quantity should always be made first to allow for any variation later that may be desired. For this reason only approximate quantities are given in the recipes, and these should be added a little at a time until the flavour satisfies you. It is easy to add more, but quite impossible to take it out.

Ketchups will be thicker when cold than whilst still hot, so don't boil down too much or it will be difficult to get out of the bottles.

BLACKBERRY KETCHUP

Simmer from five to ten pounds of blackberries in just enough water to cover them for half an hour or until quite soft. Strain them through a sieve or butter-muslin, pressing out as much pulp as possible.

Measure this juice, and for each pint have ready about half a teaspoonful of salt, one teaspoonful of sugar, half a teaspoonful of ground mustard, a little cinnamon, ground cloves and nutmeg (half a teaspoonful to three pints) and half a pint of vinegar.

Replace the strained juice in the preserving pan and simmer, gradually adding the spices and vinegar until the flavour is right. Then simmer for a further ten minutes, fill into heated bottles and close immediately. Alternatively, allow the mixture to cool, then fill into bottles and sterilize at 170° F.

This last method will allow you to know if the ketchup will be too thick when cold or needs further boiling down.

CRANBERRY KETCHUP

Cranberry ketchup is made in the same way as blackberry ketchup, by preparing a pulp first. Take five pounds of sound, unbruised cranberries, add enough water to just cover the fruit and simmer till quite soft, breaking up the fruit by stirring and mashing with a wooden spoon. Strain the pulp through a sieve or muslin and return to the preserving pan.

Add to this about one pint of vinegar, two pounds of sugar, two ounces of salt, one teaspoonful of ground allspice, half a teaspoonful of ground ginger, half a teaspoonful of cinnamon and half a teaspoonful of cayenne pepper, and possibly a little clove if the flavour is liked.

Simmer until fairly thick, then either bottle hot or allow to cool and bottle, subsequently sterilizing in the bottles.

Cranberry ketchup is favoured in America with hot or cold turkey and other wild-fowl.

ELDERBERRY KETCHUP

An early edition of *Domestic Cookery* gives a recipe for an elderberry ketchup under the title of " Pontac Ketchup," but I have been unable to find the origin of the term. The original instructions are to " bake with the bread," but as we no longer have home-made bread (more is the pity) the recipe has been slightly altered.

Take about four pounds of ripe elderberries, place them in a preserving pan and cover with vinegar. Bring them slowly to the boil and simmer for fifteen minutes, then strain off the liquor whilst still hot.

To this liquor add about a teaspoonful of peppercorns, half a teaspoonful of cloves, a teaspoonful of mace and four shallots or one onion to every quart of liquor. Bring this to the boil, and when simmering put in half a pound of anchovies to every quart and continue to simmer until the anchovies are dissolved.

In practice it was found that a tablespoonful of salt to every quart of liquor gave almost as good a result. But only almost and not quite.

Bottle whilst hot into heated bottles. It is recommended for fish.

GRAPE KETCHUP

Grape ketchup is still made in America and I have often had it in Ontario. It is excellent in the summer with cold meats, and the small sweet-water grape mentioned in a previous section is a satisfactory base.

Place five pounds of stemmed grapes in a preserving pan with one pint of vinegar, simmer for half an hour, then rub through a sieve or muslin.

To this pulp add one pound of sugar, one teaspoonful of powdered cinnamon, one teaspoonful of cloves, one teaspoonful of allspice, one teaspoonful of cayenne pepper and one table-spoonful of salt.

Continue to simmer until fairly thick, then bottle hot and close securely. Alternatively allow the ketchup to cool, then bottle and sterilize at 170° **F.**

Grape ketchup has a delicate flavour, so care must be taken in the spicing.

MUSHROOM KETCHUP

Chapter xi. of Hannah Glasse's *Domestic Cookery Made Easy* is headed " For Captains of Ships," and the first recipe is " To make catchup to keep twenty years," and is for mushrooms.

It is one of the most illuminating in the book for the home pickler and starts, " Take a gallon of strong, stale beer."

Now what does this imply ? The strong beer of those days WAS strong and, as pasteurization had not even been dreamed of, when such beer finally turned sour and became in effect vinegar it would probably have an acidity of from 6 to 8 per cent. or even higher. When to this she added a pound of anchovies, a pound of shallots and mace, pepper, ginger and cloves, then simmered the lot in a tightly covered crock until half wasted, she was actually making a high concentration of natural preservatives. Of course it would keep twenty years and she was safe in saying, " You may carry it to the Indies," especially as her final note is, " The stronger and staler the beer, the better the catchup will keep."

Nowadays beer never has a chance to be either strong or stale, and mushroom ketchup is usually made without vinegar but with a high salt content.

Select dry, full-grown mushrooms that are not bruised, break into pieces, place in layers in a deep bowl and sprinkle with salt, allowing four ounces of salt to every two pounds of mushrooms.

Let them stand in the brine for four days, stirring twice every day, then place the bowl in the oven and cook gently for three-quarters of an hour. Next strain off the liquor and measure it. To every quart of liquor add about one teaspoonful of allspice, one teaspoonful of pepper, half a teaspoonful of ginger, half a teaspoonful of mace and a little clove and cinnamon. Simmer the ketchup in a preserving pan till reduced to about half the original volume, then fill into warmed bottles and close immediately.

It is very necessary to make a trial lot—about half a pint—with the liquor to test the final flavour, as it is one of the ketchups that over-spicing can easily spoil. Some recipes add onion, shallot or garlic and other herbs, for there are many variations for mushroom ketchup.

8

TOMATO KETCHUP

Tomato ketchup has become the most popular of all commercial sauces and in this form is usually made from a thick puree prepared in factories near the farms where the tomatoes are grown.   Thousands of acres are devoted to their cultivation in America, Canada, Italy and many other countries.

It is quite easy to make at home and, as the spicing can be varied, offers an interesting change to the somewhat monotonous flavour of the commercial formulæ.

The one thing to be careful about is possible fermentation during storage, and the bottles should always be sterilized after filling at 170° F. and closed down whilst hot.

Ripe tomatoes only are used, and two different recipes are given, but your own ingenuity can have wide play with this ketchup and it can be made mild or hot in flavour.   Chilli sauce is really a very peppery tomato ketchup.

I. Tomato Ketchup

6 lbs. of ripe tomatoes.	½ teaspoonful of allspice.
1 pint of vinegar.	½ teaspoonful of cloves.
½ lb. of sugar.	½ teaspoonful of cinnamon.
1 oz. of salt.	½ teaspoonful of cayenne pepper.

Cut the tomatoes into quarters, place them in a preserving pan with the salt and vinegar and simmer until the tomatoes are quite soft and broken up.   Strain the mixture through coarse muslin or a hair sieve, then return the puree to the preserving pan and add the sugar.   Continue to simmer till the ketchup starts to thicken, and then add the spices a little at a time, stirring thoroughly, until the flavour satisfies you.   You may not want all the cayenne pepper, clove or cinnamon, so don't put the full quantities in at the start.

When the ketchup is reasonably thick, fill into hot bottles and seal immediately, or allow it to cool slightly, then fill the bottles and sterilize at 170° F. for fifteen minutes.

Remember it will be thicker when cold than hot, so don't reduce it too far.

2. Tomato Ketchup

12 ripe tomatoes.	2 teaspoonsful of clove.
2 onions finely chopped.	2 teaspoonsful of cinnamon.
1 pint of vinegar.	2 teaspoonsful of allspice.
3 tablespoonsful of sugar.	2 teaspoonsful of grated nutmeg.
1 tablespoonful of salt.	½ teaspoonful of cayenne pepper.

Cut the tomatoes into quarters and chop the onion finely, then put all the ingredients into a preserving pan, bring to the boil and cook slowly for two and a half hours. Through very coarse muslin strain out the tomato skins, fill into bottles and sterilize at 170° F. for fifteen minutes, and close whilst hot.

WALNUT KETCHUP

Walnut ketchup, like pickled walnuts, must be made before the shell has hardened, which is not later than the first week of July.

Select from eighty to one hundred green walnuts, cut them in half and crush them, then place them in a deep jar or crock.

Now prepare the following pickle. To two quarts of vinegar add one pound of chopped onion, half a pound of salt, one ounce of peppercorns, half an ounce of allspice, half a teaspoonful of cloves and half a teaspoonful of nutmeg. Bring this to the boil and pour over the crushed walnuts, and allow the mixture to stand for two weeks, stirring each day. Then drain off the liquor, place it in the preserving pan and simmer for about an hour.

Fill into heated bottles and close immediately. Like all ketchups, the spicing can be varied to suit your own taste.

Section Four

PICKLED FISH
AND MEATS

PICKLED FISH AND MEATS

" Have you ever tried kippers cold ?
What ! with vinegar ? "

*Rt. Hon. Winston Churchill, First Lord
of the Admiralty.*

A GREAT Frenchman once remarked of the English that
they boasted a hundred dishes but only one sauce, and this
could be said with even greater truth to-day about our
neglect of fish. Possessing probably the finest sea-harvest
in the world, we seem to be rapidly reducing our fish diet
to the vapid monotony of fried fish and chips !

Official figures tell a discouraging tale. With herrings
alone, over 80 per cent. of the catch was exported before
the 1914–1918 war, chiefly to the Baltic countries, where
they fully realize the value of this delicious food, whilst
during the last twenty years the home consumption has
fallen by 45 per cent.

Yet herrings are one of the cheapest and most nutritious
foods we have, rich in protein, fat and vitamins A and D,
and it has the advantage over mutton in price, that is
weight for weight of food value, of less than half.

What is the explanation of this neglect? Undoubtedly the decline of fish pickling at home has something to do with it. *Domestic Cookery*, so popular only a hundred years ago, gives recipes for making imitation pickled sturgeon, for which she uses " a fine large turkey but not too old "; three ways of pickling salmon; pickled mackerel, which she calls " Caveach "; potting and pickling herrings and sprats; and two ways of pickling oysters!

Have you ever tried pickled salmon or Caveach or even soused herrings? No; fish and chips, please! But do you ever consider that under its nice brown overcoat of fried bread-crumbs your plaice or sole or whiting may be the humble dog-fish in masquerade? For fish, bread-crumbs are like Charity—they cover a multitude of sins!

Admittedly we cannot to-day take the advice of the author of *Domestic Cookery* and insist on buying Thames salmon, which she says is best and " bears the highest price "; but what about mackerel and herrings? Ah! you say, the bones!

Certainly the herring, blessed with so much goodness, is cursed with a double quantity of skeleton, but when pickled or soused this quickly disappears, for the vinegar soon settles the bones in the same way that they are not present in tinned herrings and sardines, for fish bones are composed almost entirely of lime, which the vinegar dissolves.

All fish can be pickled, either for storage or for immediate use, but not all pickle as well as the herring.

Here, therefore, we shall deal chiefly with this fish, as it is available for three parts of the year, is cheap and simple to prepare; whilst such things as salmon and trout, though they were fairly common articles of food a hundred years ago when the population was smaller and our rivers less polluted, are to-day comparatively luxury dishes. Yet even with these there is one point of interest: frozen salmon, of which large quantities are imported, and which is the base of so much smoked salmon, is excellent pickled or soused.

There is one important difference between pickling fish and vegetables. Fish contain much less water—it varies between 50 and 70 per cent. as against the vegetables' 90 per cent.—and so vinegar of such high acidity is not necessary. Indeed, in sousing it is usual to dilute with about one-third of water, as otherwise the fish may taste too sharp. This does not apply, however, in the pickling of raw fish for keeping, where the 3 per cent. rule still holds as for vegetable pickles.

HERRINGS

Anyone who has travelled in Scandinavia will be familiar with the many ways Herrings can be treated. Dried, smoked, salted, steeped in oil, pickled in vinegar or soused, as well as the ordinary grilling and boiling, they are eaten in really astonishing quantity, and when you realize that they have probably been caught by Scottish or Yarmouth fishermen, the inevitable question arises, " Why can't I get them like this at home ? " The answer is that you can, but you won't take the trouble !

So when the herring harvest next comes round—and it starts in May and goes on till the following New Year—try some of these recipes.

DEVILLED HERRINGS. Strictly speaking these are not pickled at all, but the recipe is given because you can use some of the chutneys in their preparation.

Clean and gut the fish and take out the roes, but keep those that are soft. Soak the fish in vinegar for two hours, adding a teaspoonful of salt. Next stuff each fish with any of the hotter chutneys (an Indian pickle is excellent), mixing in the soft roes with the chutney.

Then fry in a hot pan, having well peppered the outside of the fish first. This is a good way of treating the fresh herring, as it not only overcomes much of the bone problem but you can vary the flavours with different chutneys.

SPICED HERRING FILLETS. These are the same as Rollmops except that the fish is filleted, which again the fishmonger does for you. Soak the fillets in standard brine for NOT more than two hours and give only a six-hour vinegar-bath. Fillets are much thinner than whole fish and do not need such long treatment. Finally pack them in as shallow jars as possible, a layer of fillets and a layer of sliced onion, and cover with spiced vinegar.

For fillets it adds variety if you mix your spices, making some with hot spice and some with aromatic. When serving, the addition of a thinly sliced tomato is a useful garnishing.

ROLLMOPS.   These are the uncooked pickled herrings served as hors d'œuvres in hotels and restaurants.   They are quite easy to make at home, and will keep for some weeks after pickling.

Select even-sized herrings, not too large ; take off the head ; scale, gut and clean and take out the backbone, all of which you can probably persuade your fishmonger to do much easier for you.

Soak the prepared fish in a standard brine for two hours, then transfer to an unspiced vinegar-bath that will just cover them. Leave them in this for twelve hours.

In the meantime shred fairly large onions across the grain so that it is in long threads, not chopped, and when the fish are ready, roll them, starting from the head end, round a tablespoon-ful of the onion.   When you reach the tail, fasten it securely with a sharpened match or toothpick.   Pack the rolls, not too tightly, in jars, and cover with aromatic spiced vinegar.   A few whole chillies, bay leaves or a slice of lemon added to each jar will improve the appearance and flavour.   They are ready to eat in two or three days, and will keep for six weeks or more in a cool place, or for months if you possess a refrigerator.

SOUSED HERRINGS. Of the many ways there are for serving herrings, sousing is one of the best. Actually it is pickling them in vinegar for immediate consumption in the same way that beetroot is pickled, and there are many recipes for doing it. Sometimes the fish are cooked and then pickled, or they may be cooked in the actual pickle. Three different methods are given :

1. Clean, head and scale the herring, and put back all soft roes. Salt and pepper the inside, then grill the fish until just cooked through, but don't overcook.

Transfer to a flat dish, the bottom of which is covered with thinly sliced onion. Lay the fish on this and cover with hot spiced vinegar, preferably a mixed spice. Add bay leaves, slices of lemon, whole chillies or any other adornment your fancy suggests. Cover the dish and leave until quite cold, then serve.

2. After cleaning and scaling, boil the fish in a weak brine (half standard strength) for about a quarter of an hour. Allow them to drain, then place them, head to tail, in a shallow glass or earthenware dish.

Add to sufficient vinegar to cover them, shredded onion—one onion to every four fish—bay leaves, chillies and cloves, and bring to the boil. Pour over the fish and cover. Stand until cold before serving.

3. Clean and scale the fish and remove roes. Pack in the dish in which they will be served, head to tail, with the roes in between on a layer of onion and with a few bay leaves. Cover with spiced vinegar and place in the oven and cook gently for half an hour or more, until the fish are tender. Keep the dish covered whilst cooking. Let them get quite cold before serving.

In all these cases the vinegar used should be diluted with half or one-third water, and it is much better to prepare them the day before they are wanted for the table.

There are many variants of these recipes and the herbs can be used to advantage. Thyme, sorrel, sage, fennel and chives are all possible flavourings, whilst soused herrings go well with many salads, of which cold potato salad is not to be despised. In a really cool larder or refrigerator they will keep for some days.

Most of the old cookery books give recipes for potting fish for long storage. Mrs. Glasse gives one " to pickle or bake mackrel, to keep all the year," and incidentally throws an interesting light on the kitchen hygiene of those times when she adds, " but you must not put in your hands to take out the mackrel." To-day these are of only academic interest, as we can get fresh fish all the year round, so there is little need to pot for long storage.

To give all the different ways there are for pickling various fish would need a much larger volume than this little book, but mackerel, sprats, smelts and pilchards can be treated like herrings, and with equal success. The white fish and flat fish do not pickle so well, probably because of their lower fat content, and they are usually dried or salted for preservation. Still, if you get no further than realising the possibilities of a soused herring, this chapter will not have been written in vain.

MEATS

Pickled meats are of little interest to the housewife to-day. For one thing, to be successful they must be large joints, and the large joint went out of fashion with the large family. Farmers still pickle their own hams, and one occasionally meets spiced round of beef in some country inn, whilst pickled pork and salt beef can be got from the local butcher. But in case you really want to try it, here is an old recipe for spiced beef:

1 lb. salt.	½ lb. sugar.
2 oz. saltpetre.	½ lb. molasses.
½ oz. allspice.	¼ oz. peppercorns.
¼ oz. cloves.	½ pint vinegar.
4 bay leaves, a sprig of thyme, marjoram and sage.	1 gill rum.

Take all the spices and pound together with the salt, then add the sugar, molasses, vinegar and rum, and heat until thoroughly mixed. Pour over the round of beef and rub in daily for at least a week, turning the meat each time. Some authorities give old ale in place of vinegar, and the longer it is in pickle in reason the better; but this sort of thing is likely to be a failure with any joint of less than ten pounds, so don't try it for a family of three.

And so we come to the end, in the hope that some slight interest in home pickling has been aroused and with a final quotation from that Queen of Housewives, Hannah Glasse:

" I shall say no more, only hope my book will answer the ends I intend it for; which is to improve the servants and save the ladies a great deal of trouble."

www.ingramcontent.com/pod-product-compliance
Ingram Content Group UK Ltd.
Pitfield, Milton Keynes, MK11 3LW, UK
UKHW020347010325
455677UK00021B/338